THE WOODLANDS

Special thanks to Ashley, my family and friends, Nickelodeon Magazine, Bento Box Entertainment, Blindwolf Studios, Ben Berntsen, and Dan Goodsell

The Woodlands by Todd Webb
www.toddbot.com

Published by Second House
www.second---house.com

ISBN 978-0-9861621-3-8

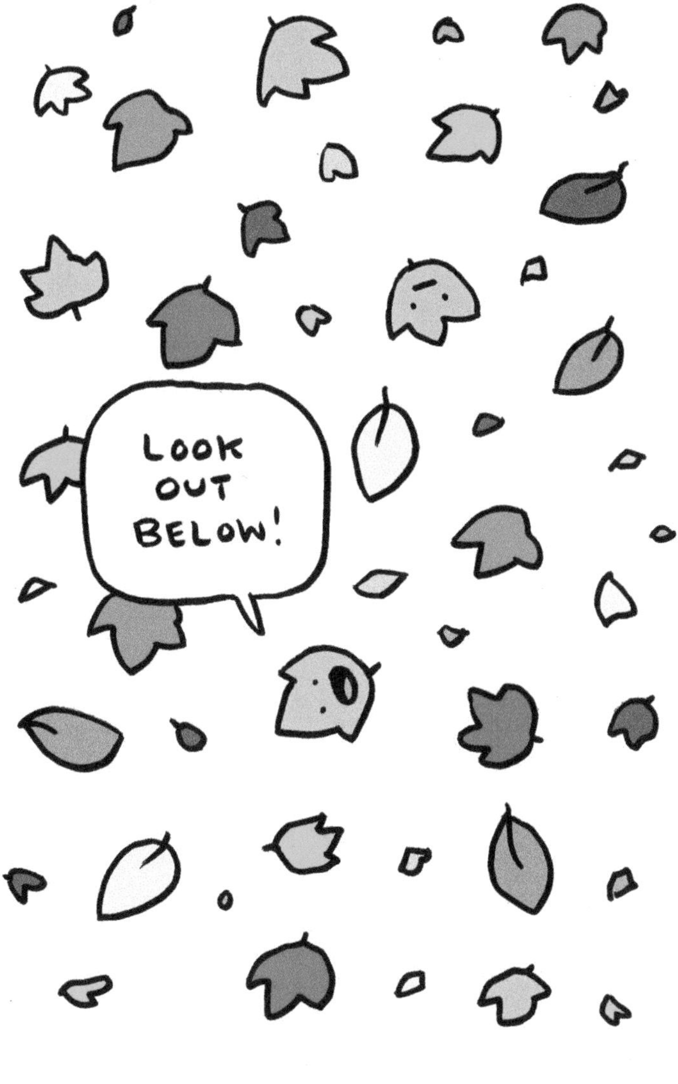
LOOK OUT BELOW!

THE WOODLANDS

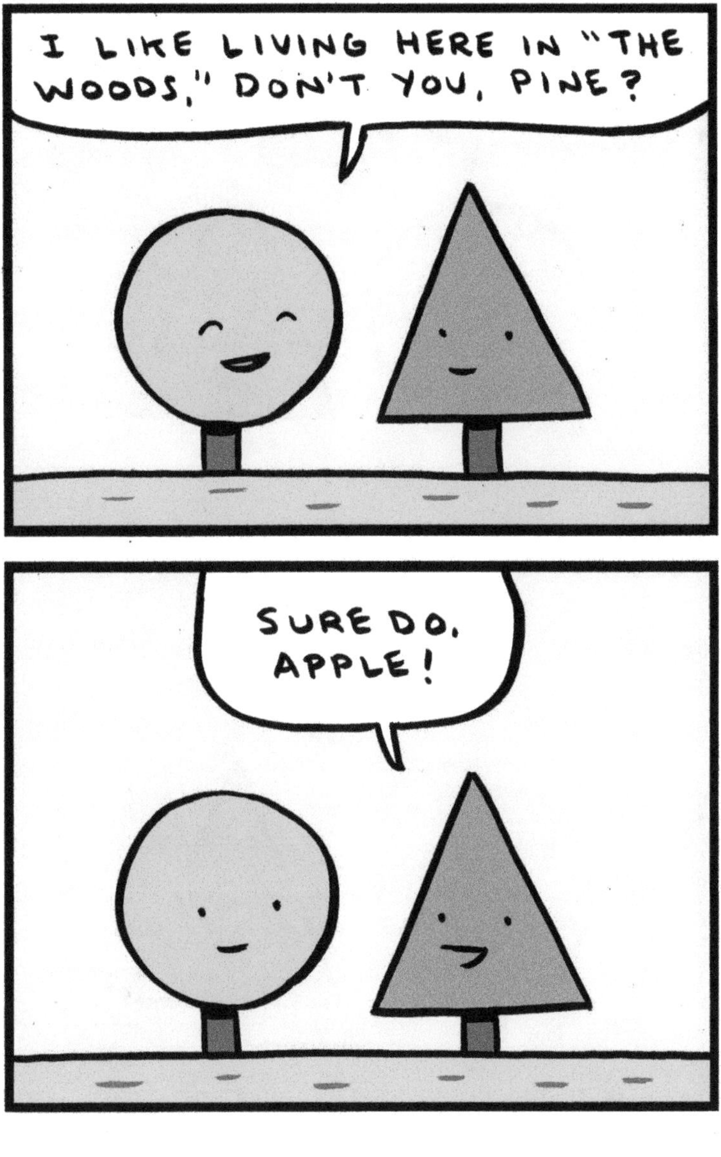
I LIKE LIVING HERE IN "THE WOODS," DON'T YOU, PINE?
SURE DO, APPLE!

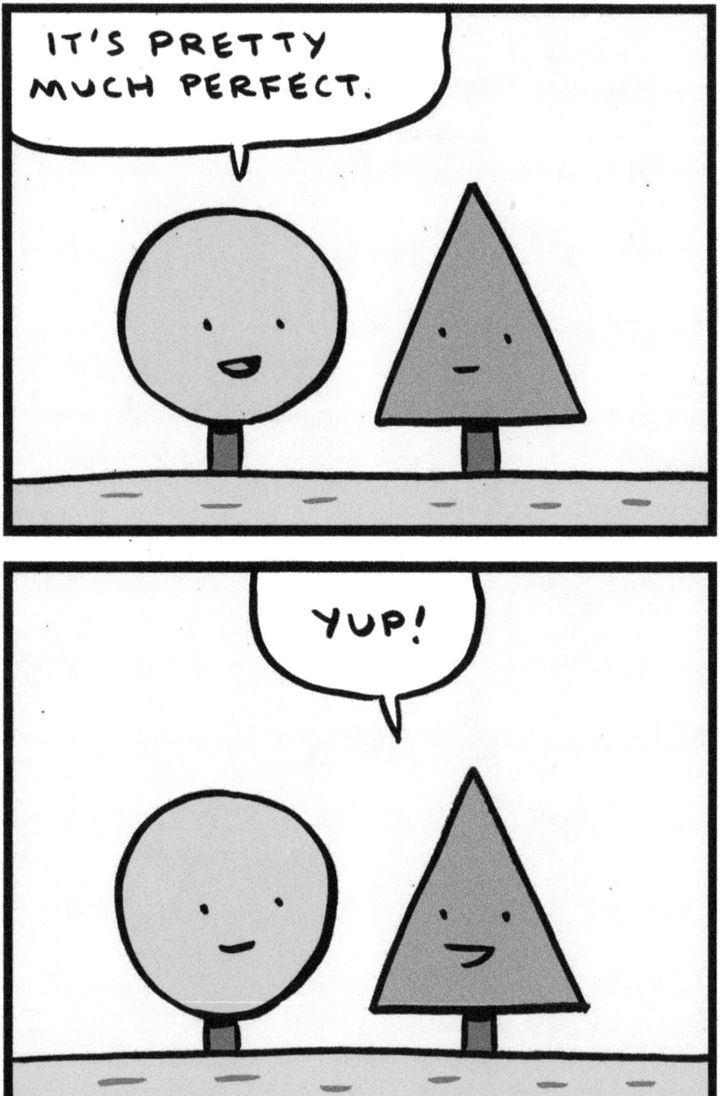
IT'S PRETTY MUCH PERFECT.
YUP!

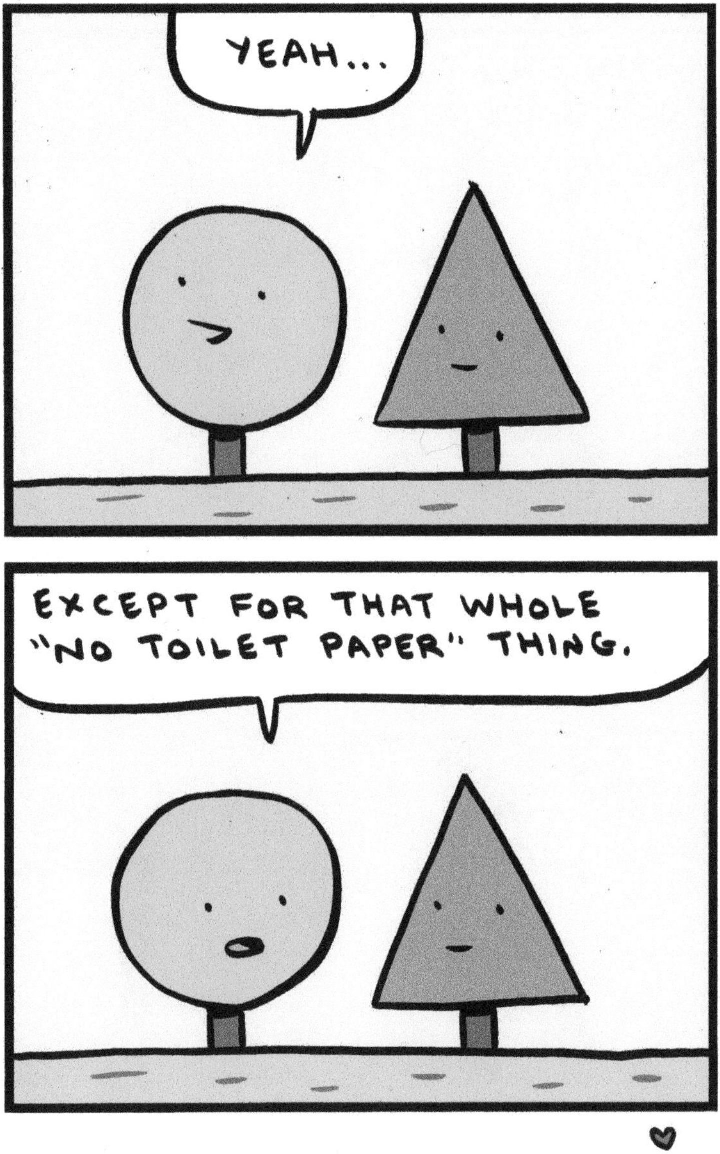
YEAH...
EXCEPT FOR THAT WHOLE "NO TOILET PAPER" THING.

DISTINGUISHED

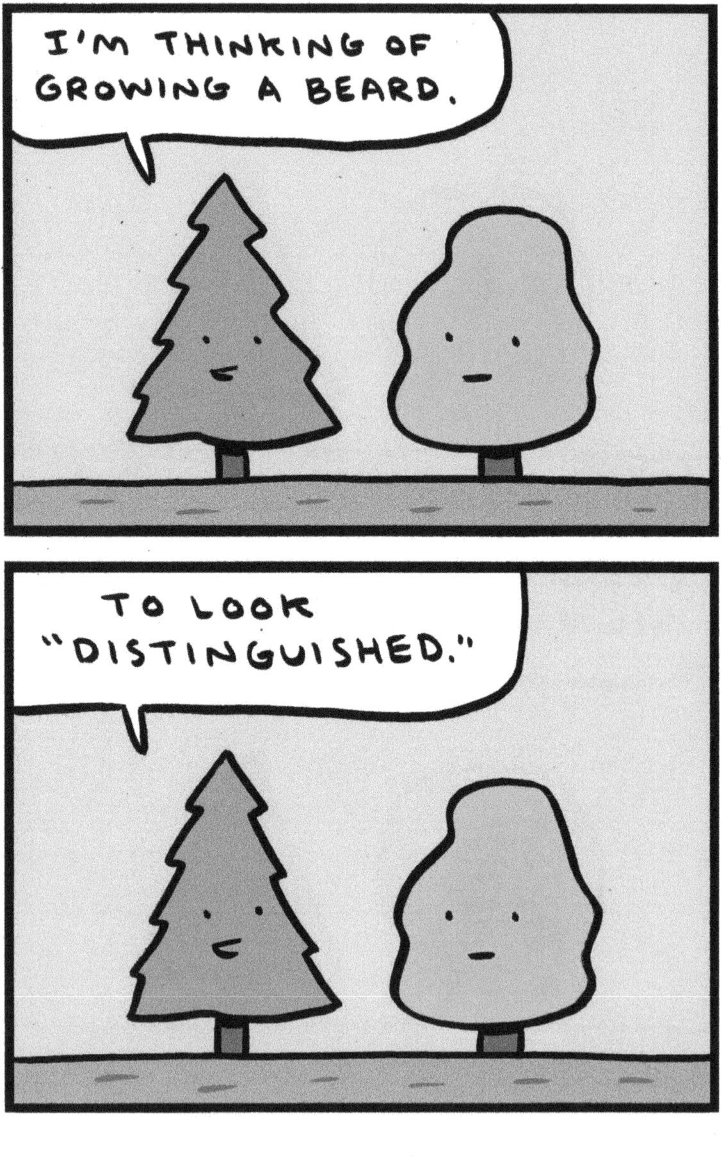
I'M THINKING OF GROWING A BEARD.
TO LOOK "DISTINGUISHED."

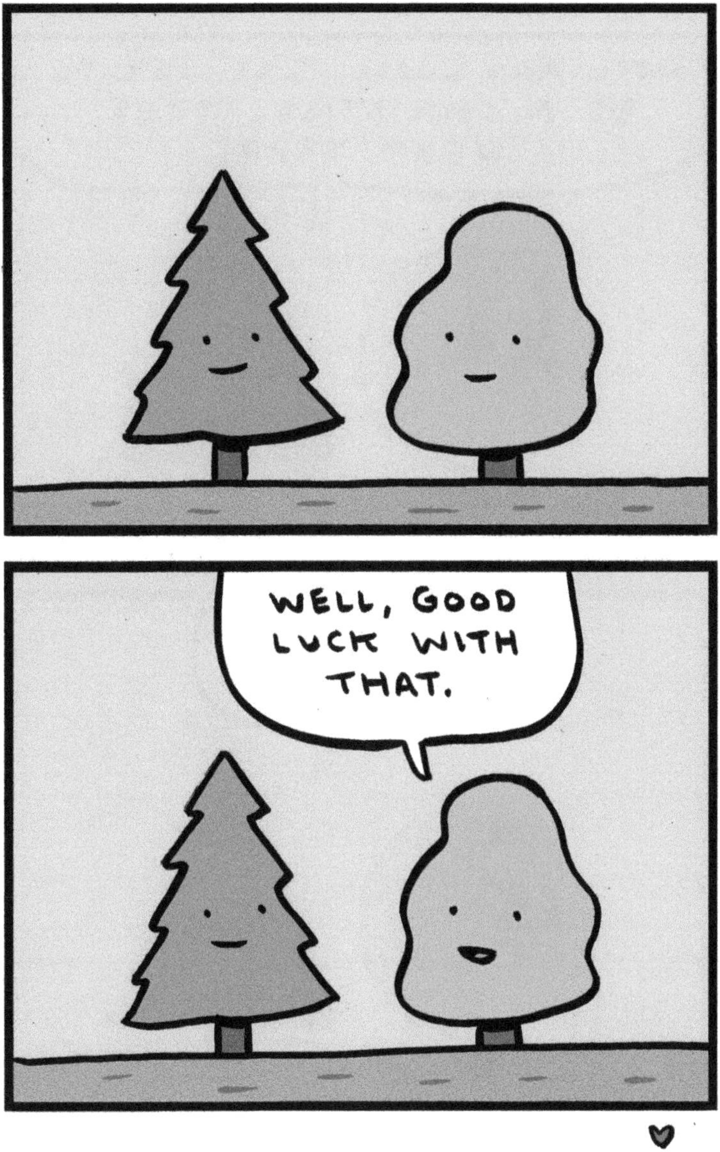
WELL, GOOD LUCK WITH THAT.

NEXT YEAR

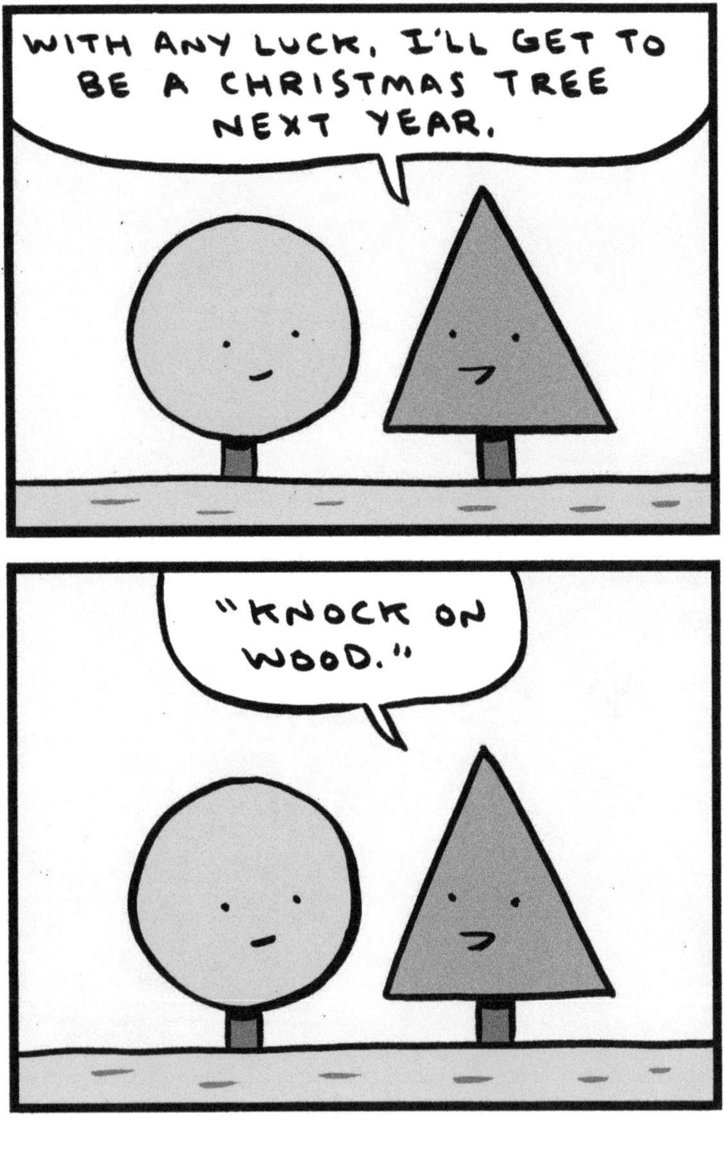
WITH ANY LUCK, I'LL GET TO BE A CHRISTMAS TREE NEXT YEAR.
"KNOCK ON WOOD."

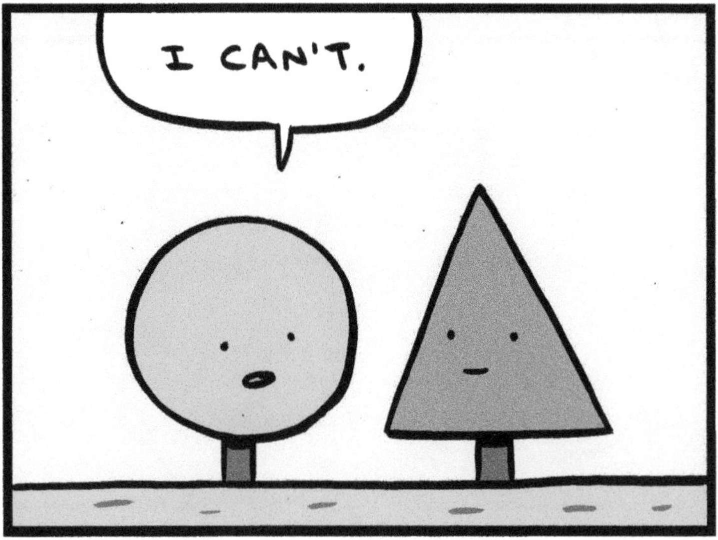
I CAN'T.

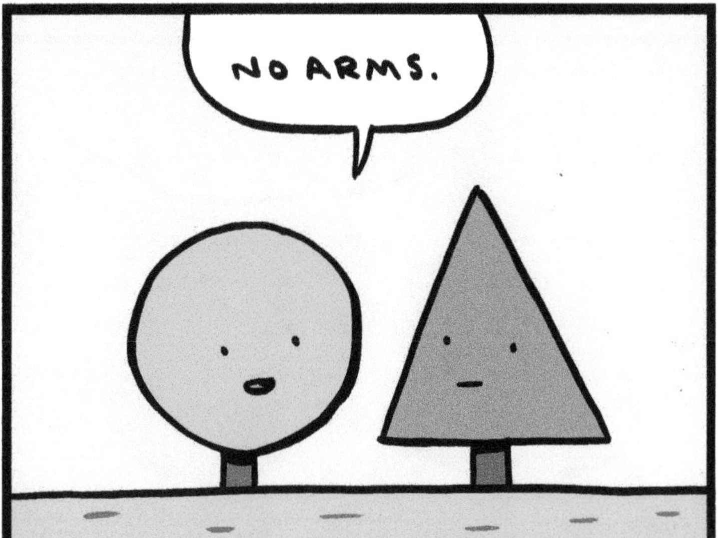
NO ARMS.

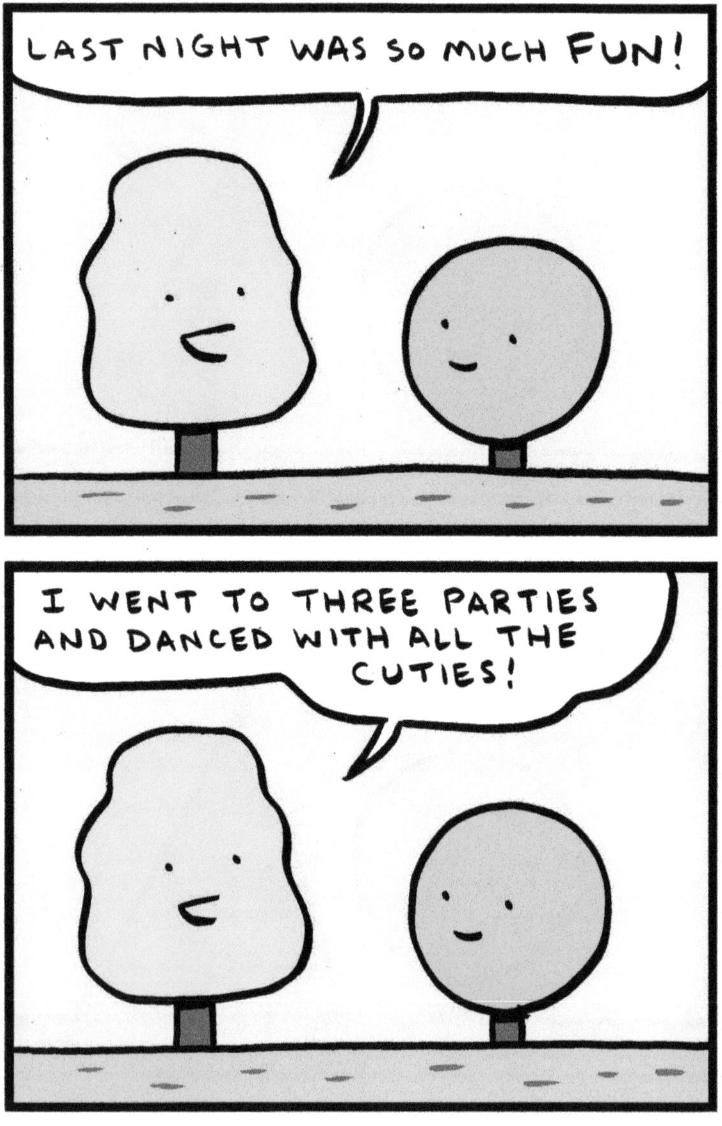
LAST NIGHT WAS SO MUCH FUN!
I WENT TO THREE PARTIES AND DANCED WITH ALL THE CUTIES!

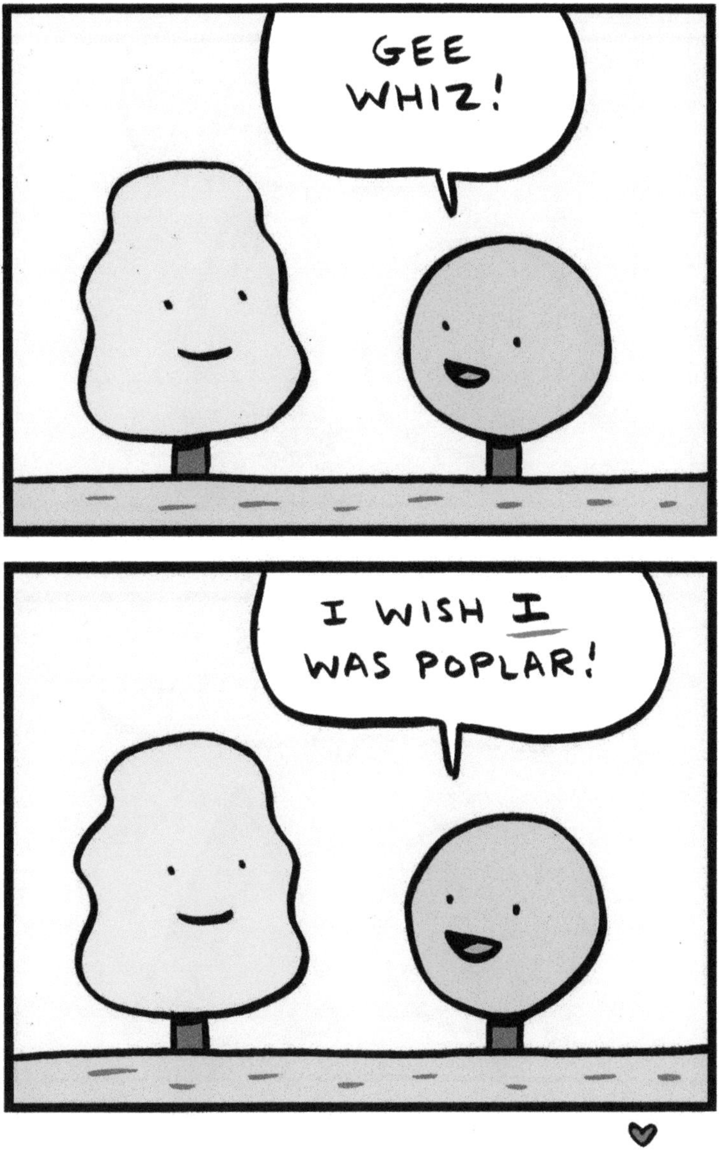
GEE WHIZ!
I WISH I WAS POPLAR!

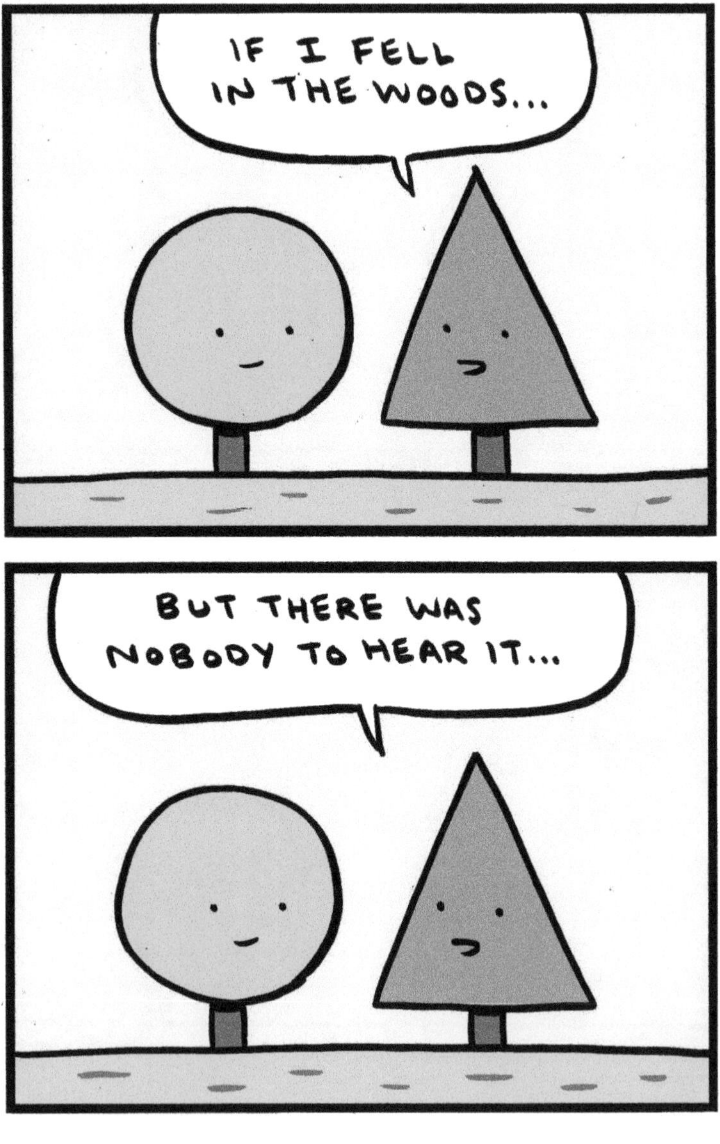
IF I FELL IN THE WOODS...
BUT THERE WAS NOBODY TO HEAR IT...

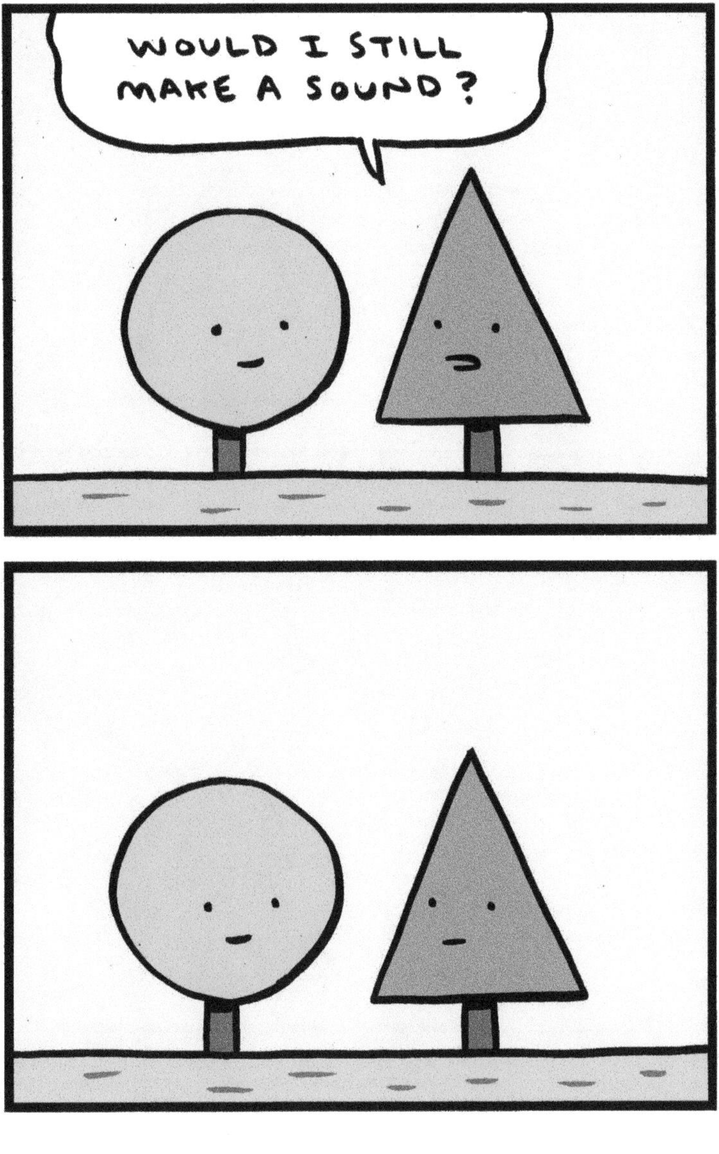
WOULD I STILL MAKE A SOUND?

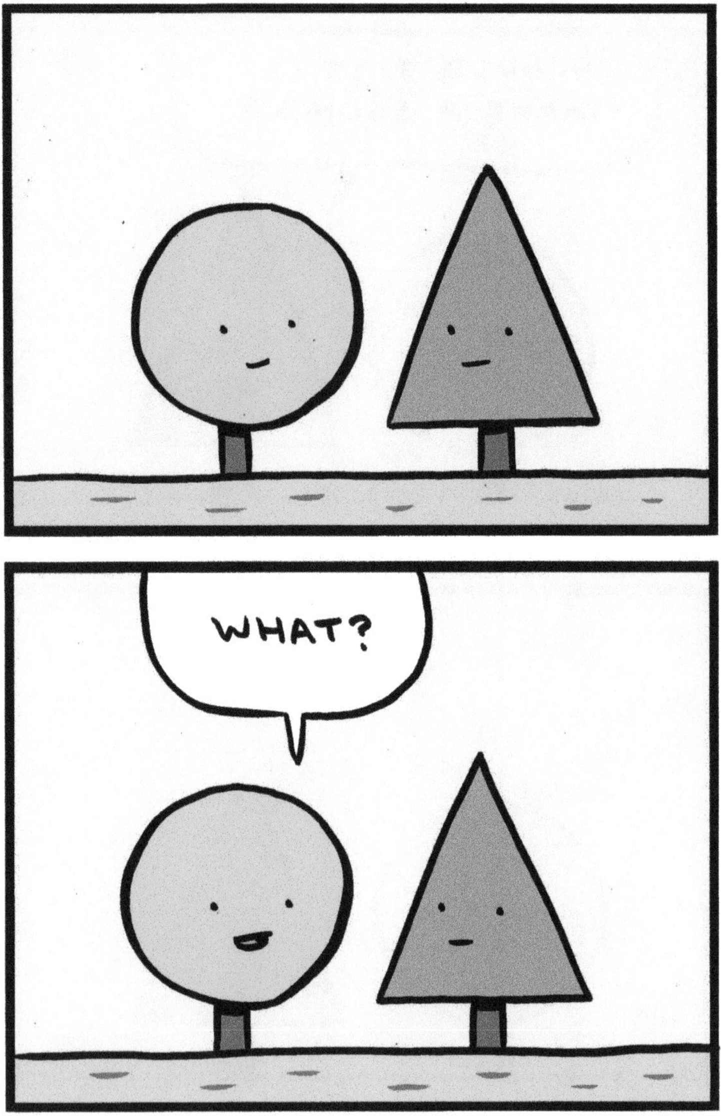
WHAT?

JEALOUSY

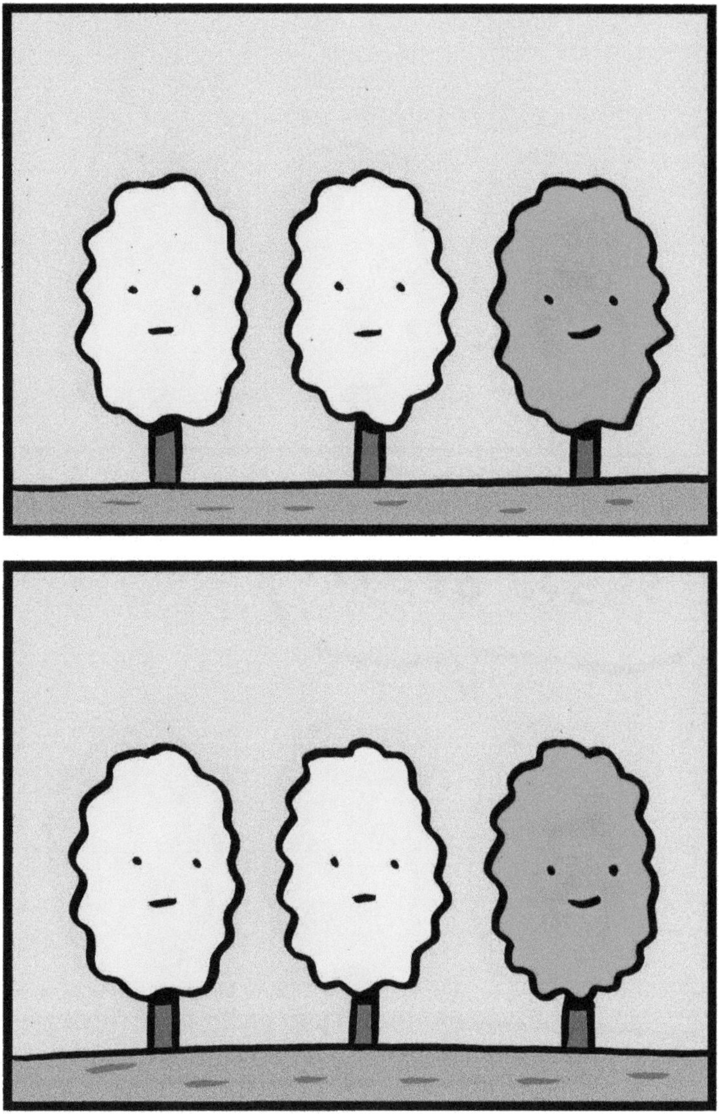

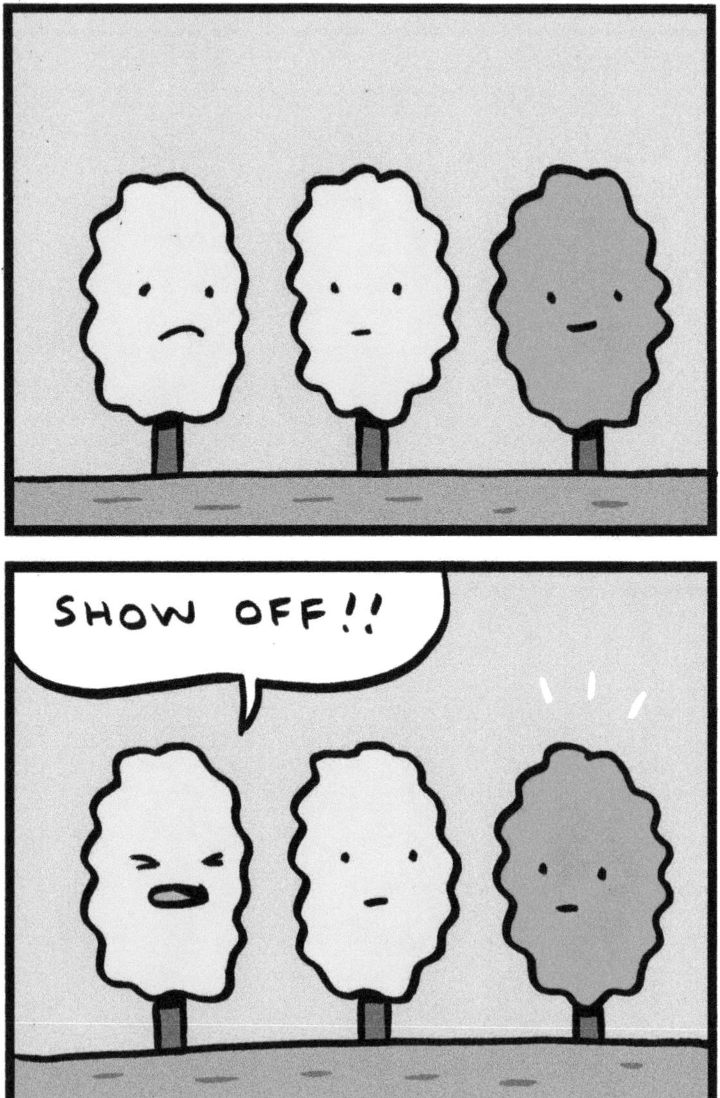
SHOW OFF!!

VACATION DESTINATION

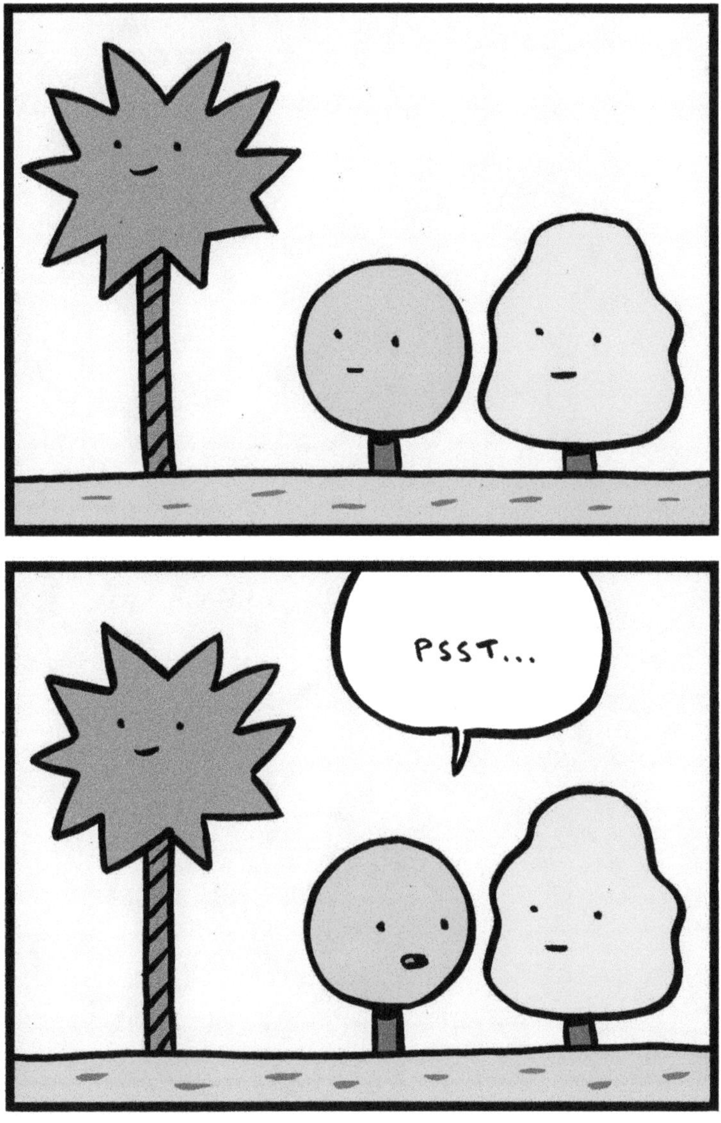
PSST...

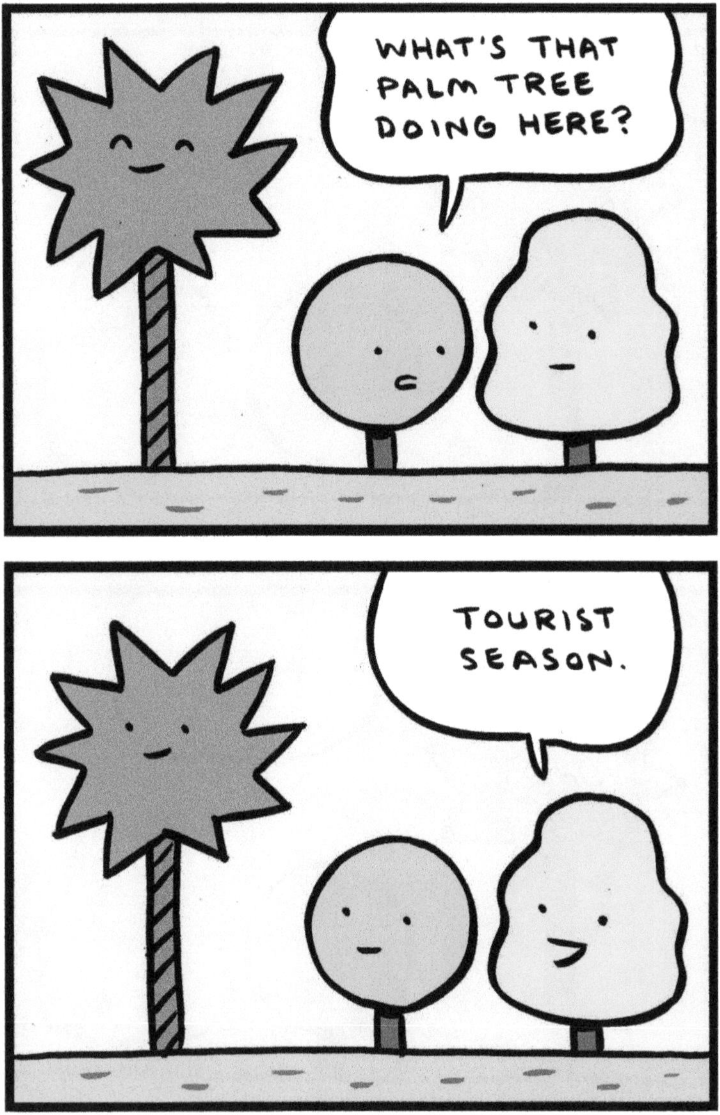
WHAT'S THAT PALM TREE DOING HERE?
TOURIST SEASON.

TICKLES

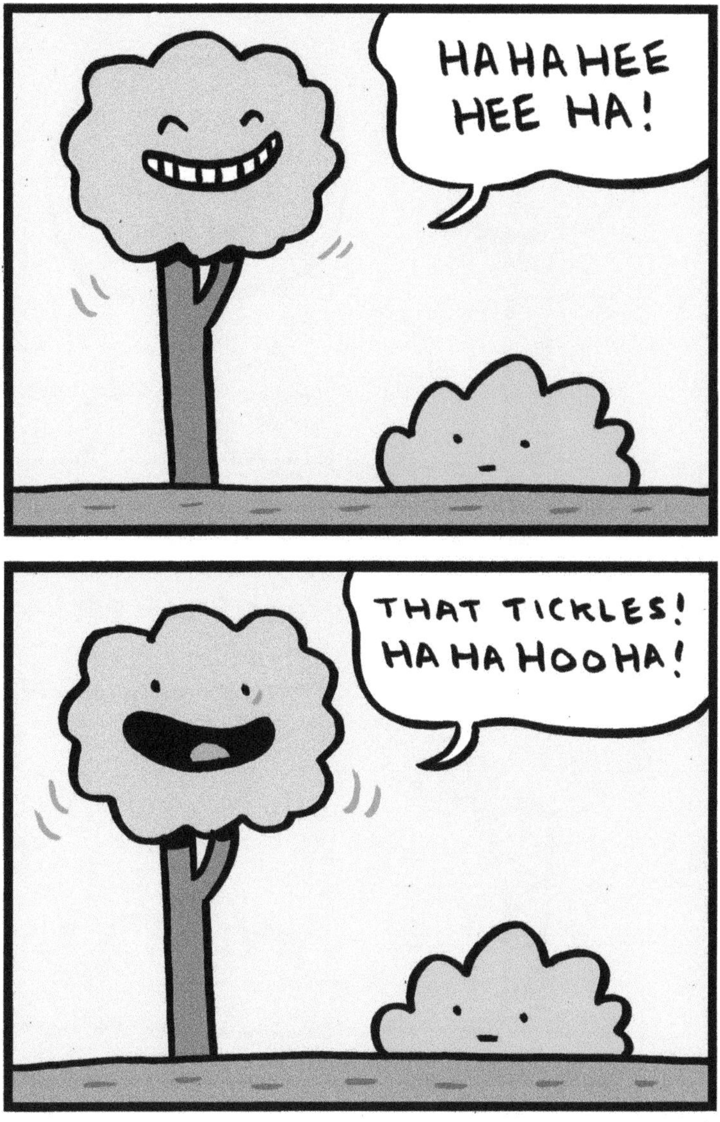
HA HA HA HEE HEE HA!
THAT TICKLES! HA HA HOO HA!

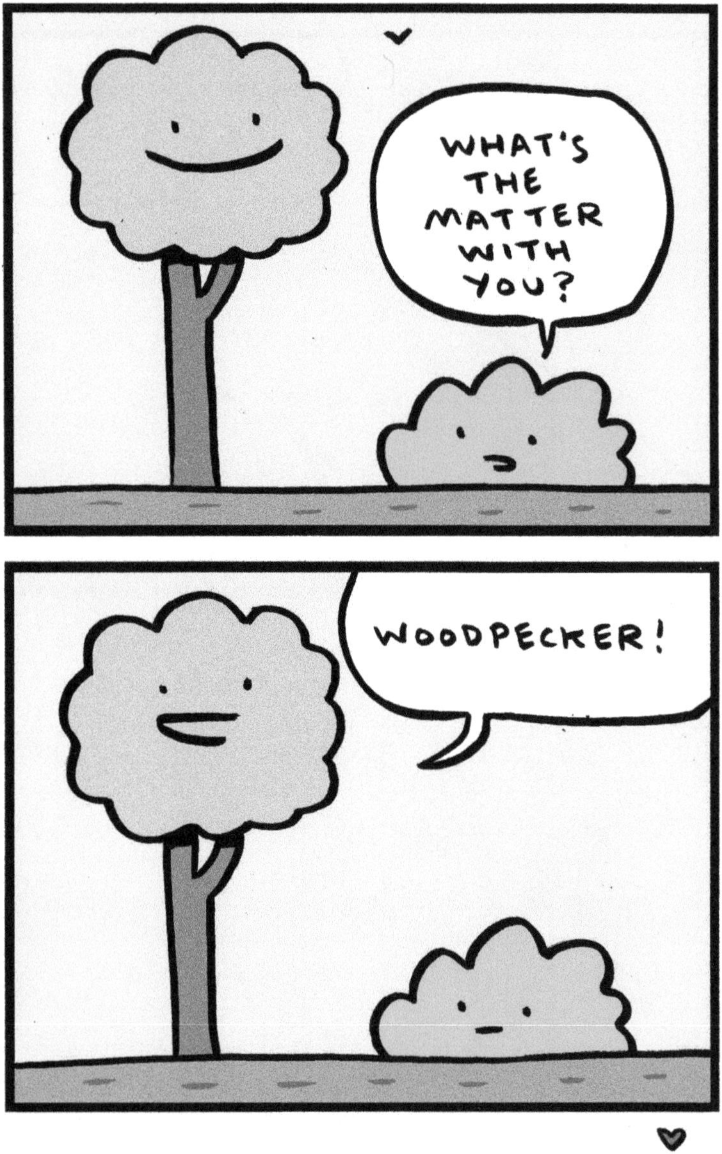
WHAT'S THE MATTER WITH YOU?
WOODPECKER!

SURPRISE

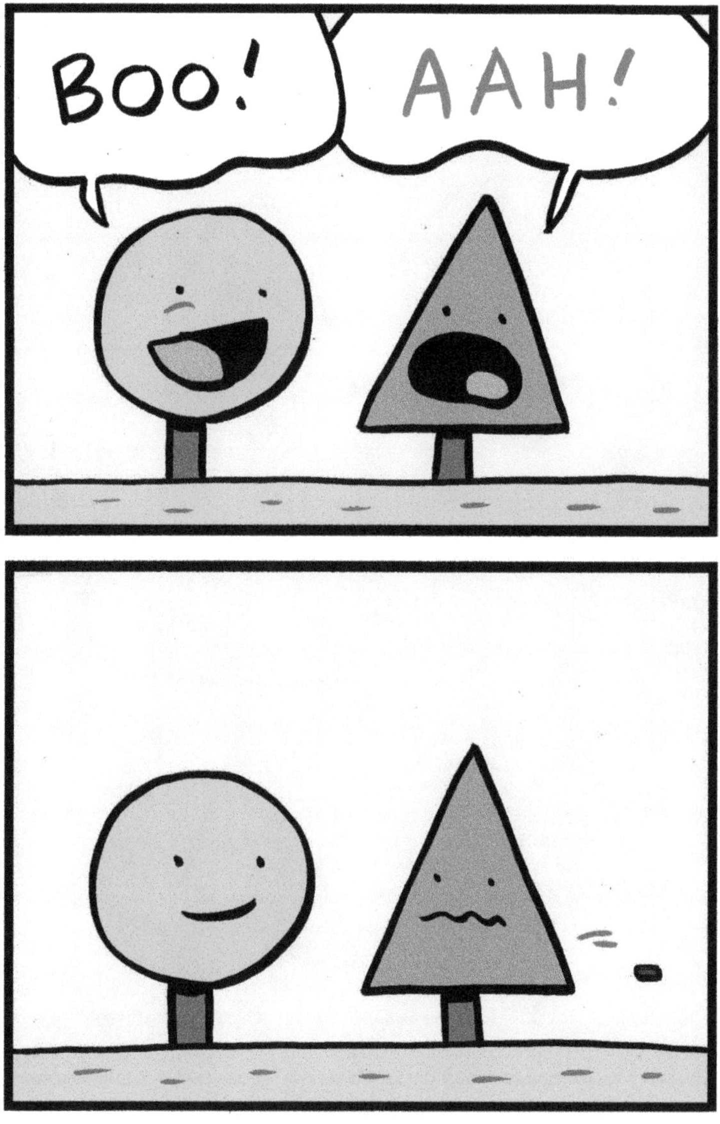
BOO!
AAH!

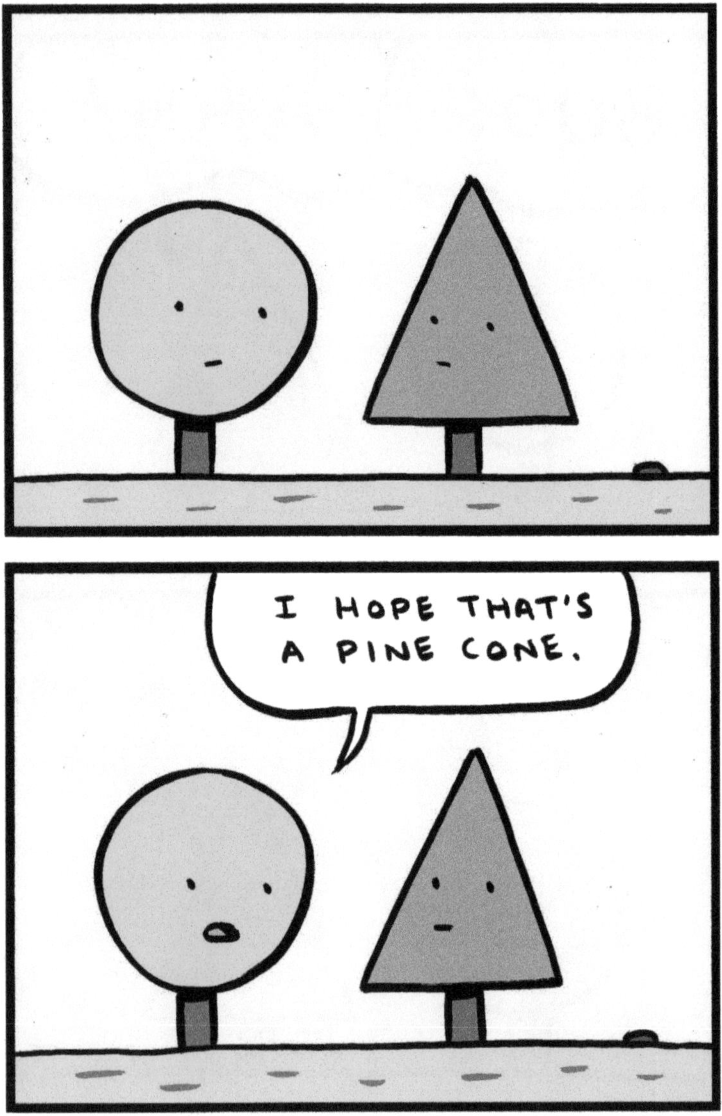
I HOPE THAT'S A PINE CONE.

WEEPING WILLOW

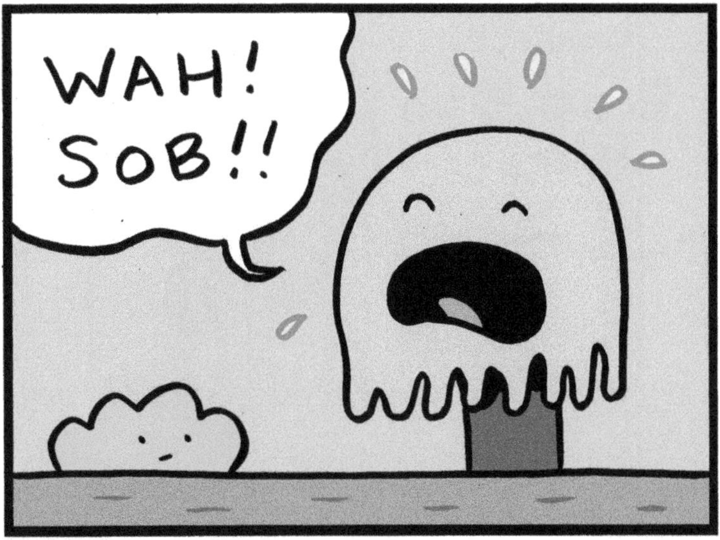
WAH! SOB!!

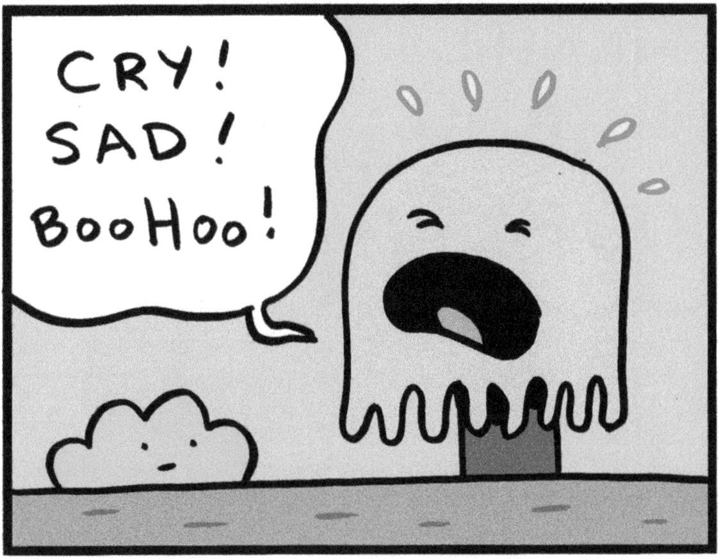
CRY! SAD! BooHoo!

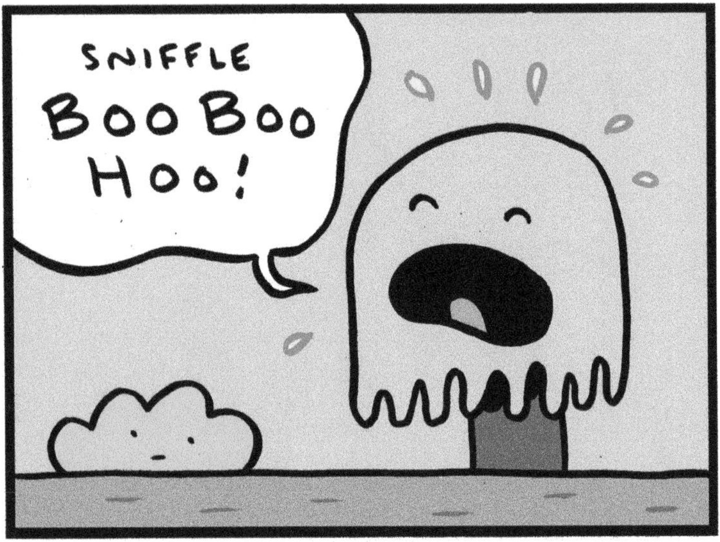
SNIFFLE
BOO BOO
HOO!

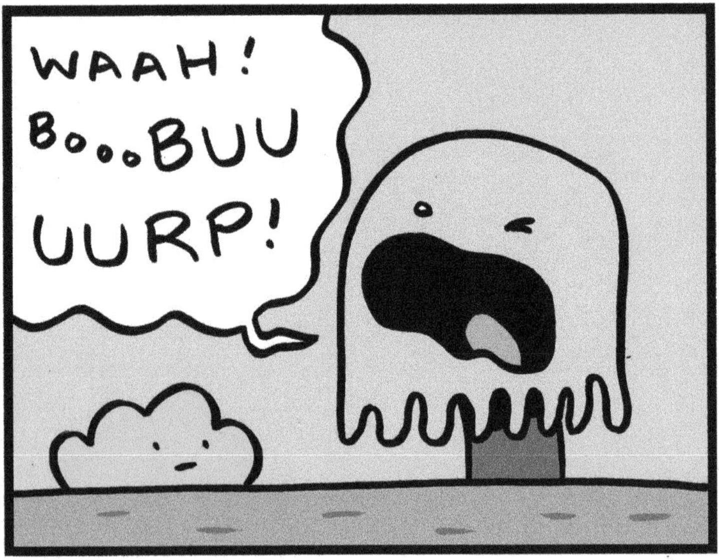
WAAH!
BoooBUU
UURP!

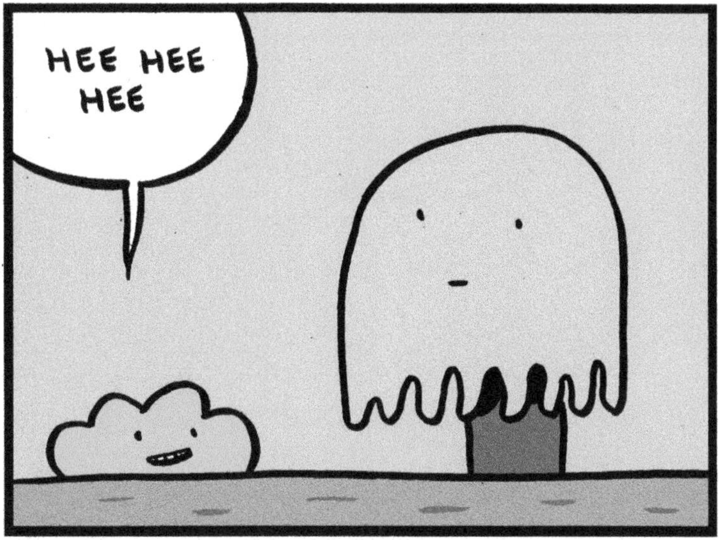
HEE HEE HEE

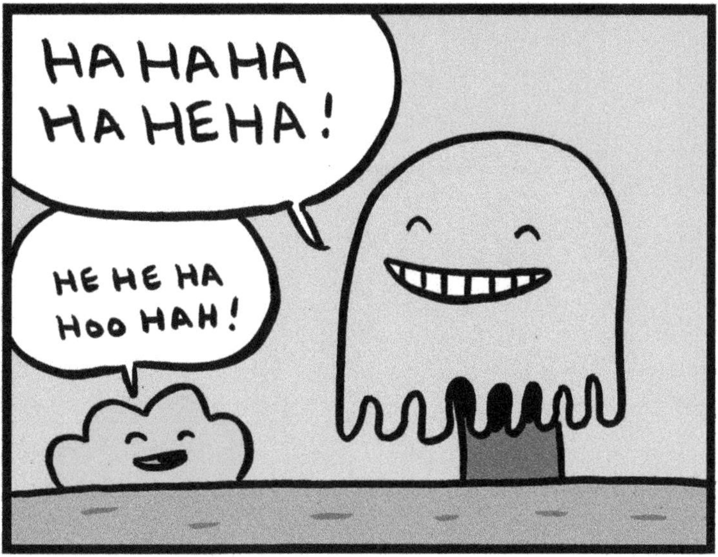
HA HA HA HA HE HA!
HE HE HA HOO HAH!

SNACK TIME

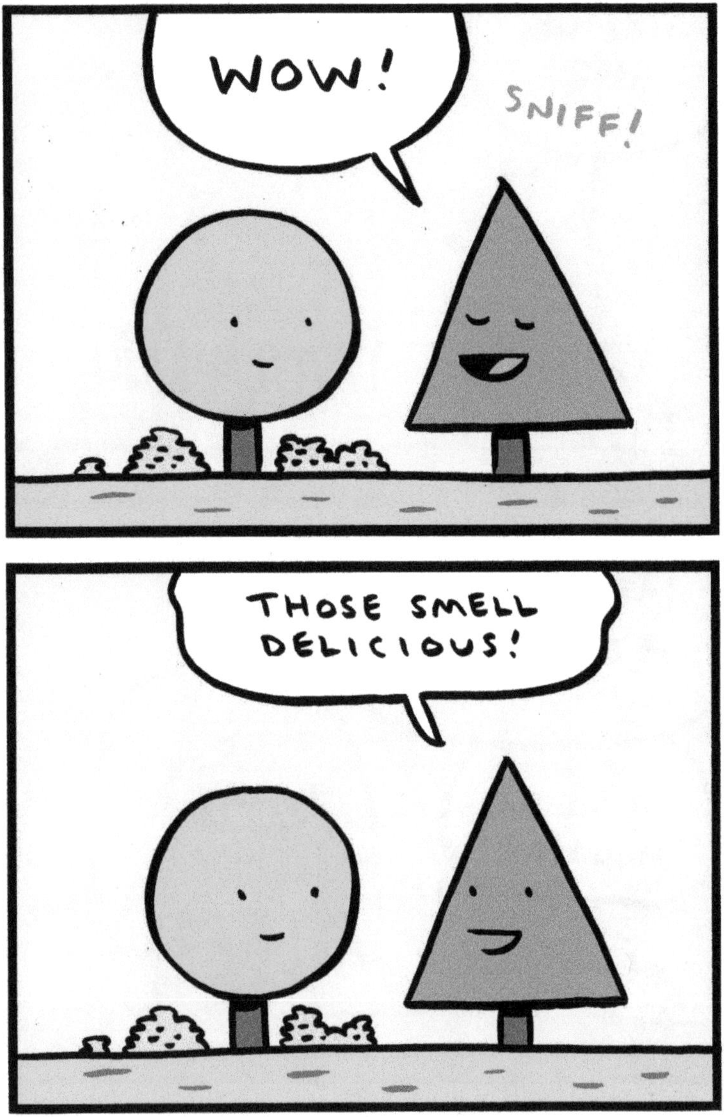
WOW!
SNIFF!
THOSE SMELL DELICIOUS!

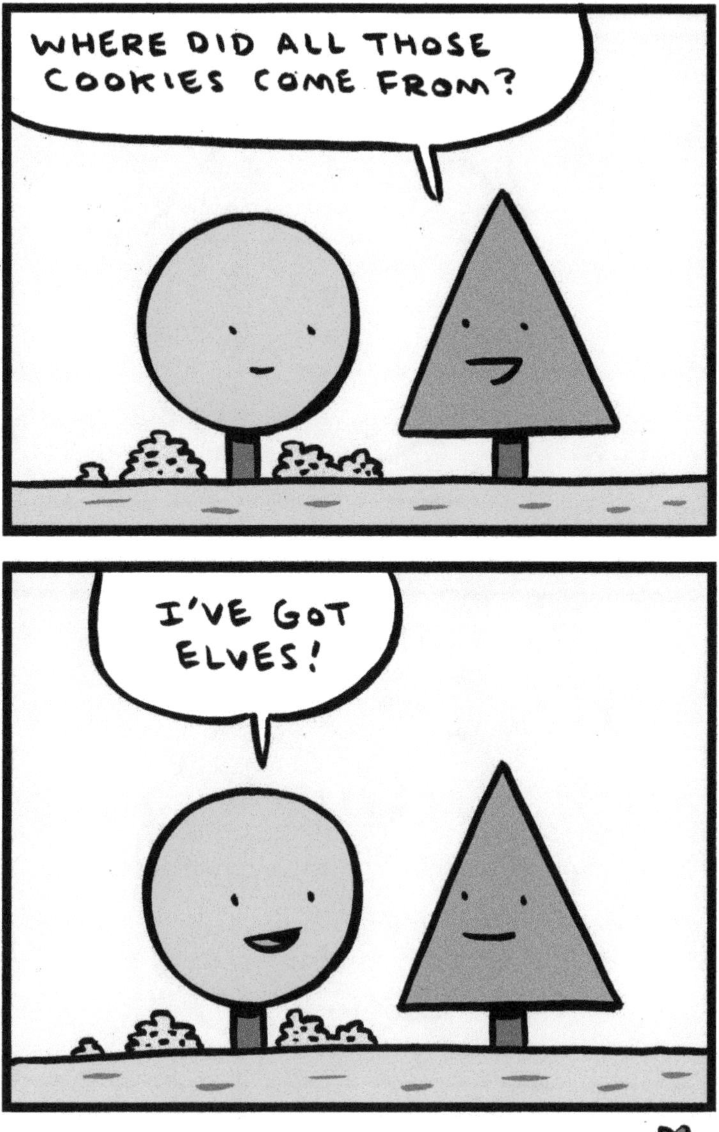
WHERE DID ALL THOSE COOKIES COME FROM?
I'VE GOT ELVES!

SEASONS

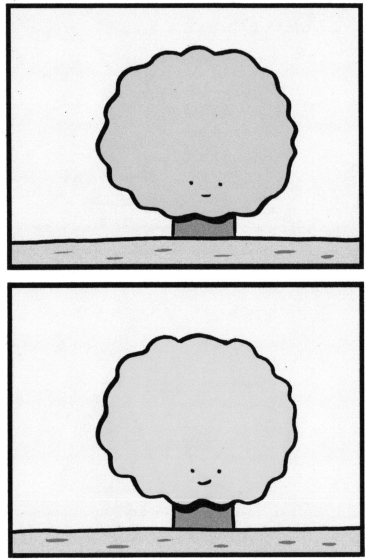

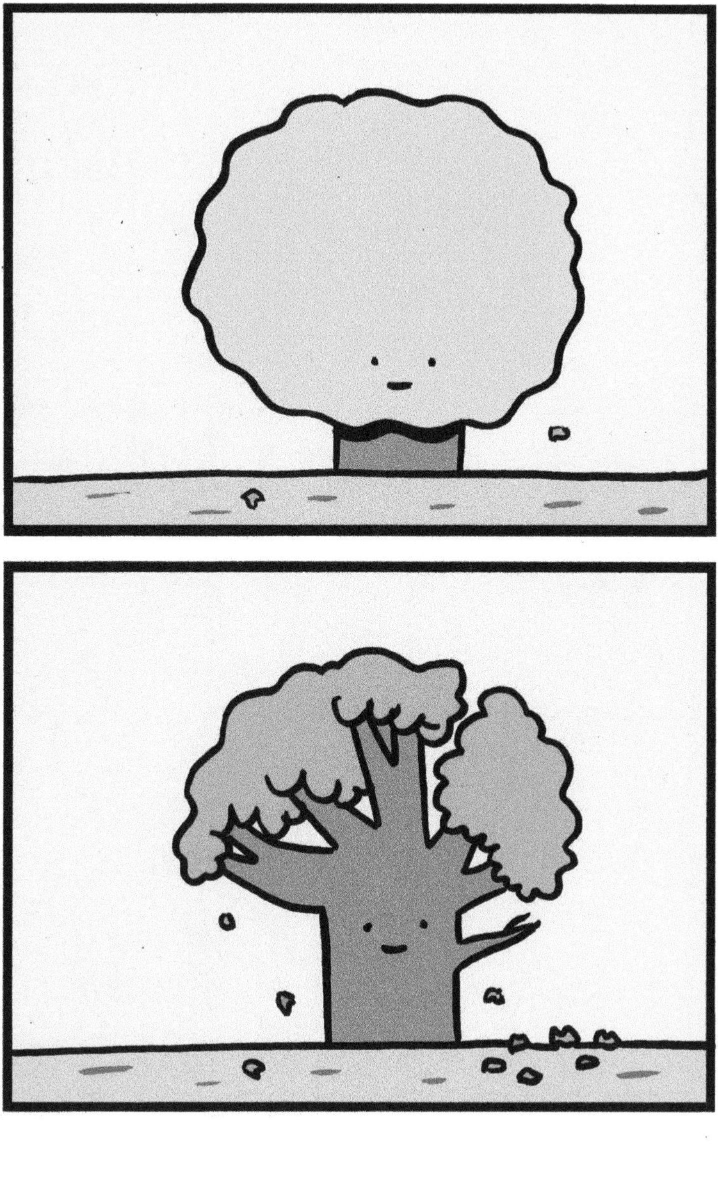

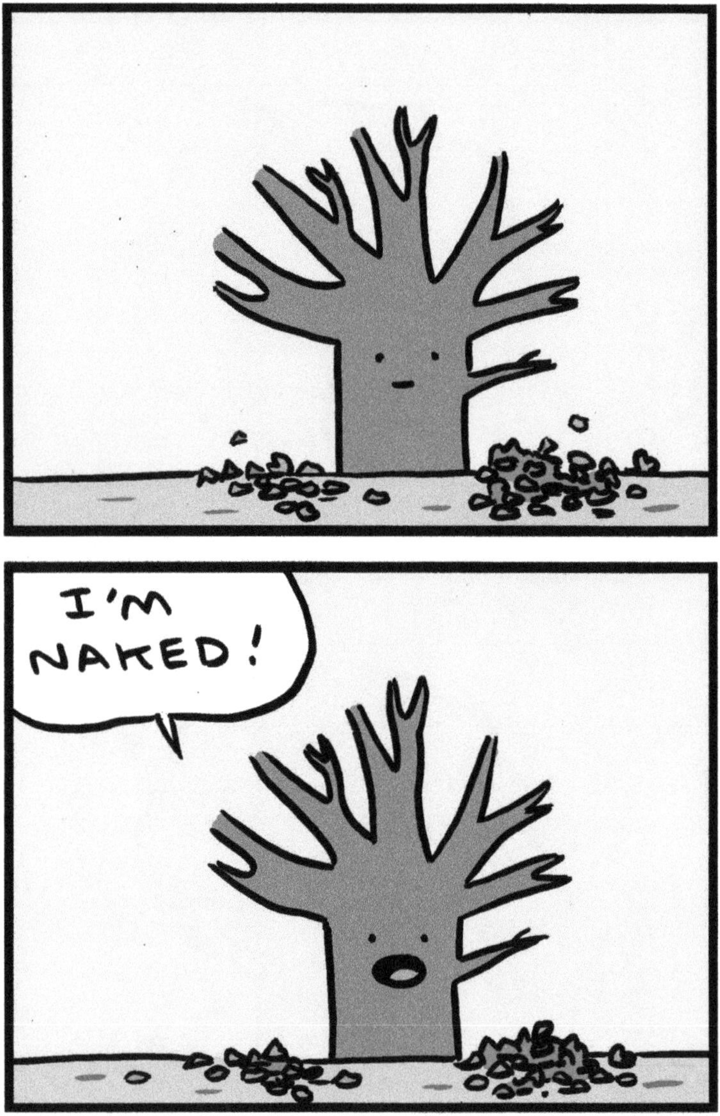
I'M NAKED!

LEWIS

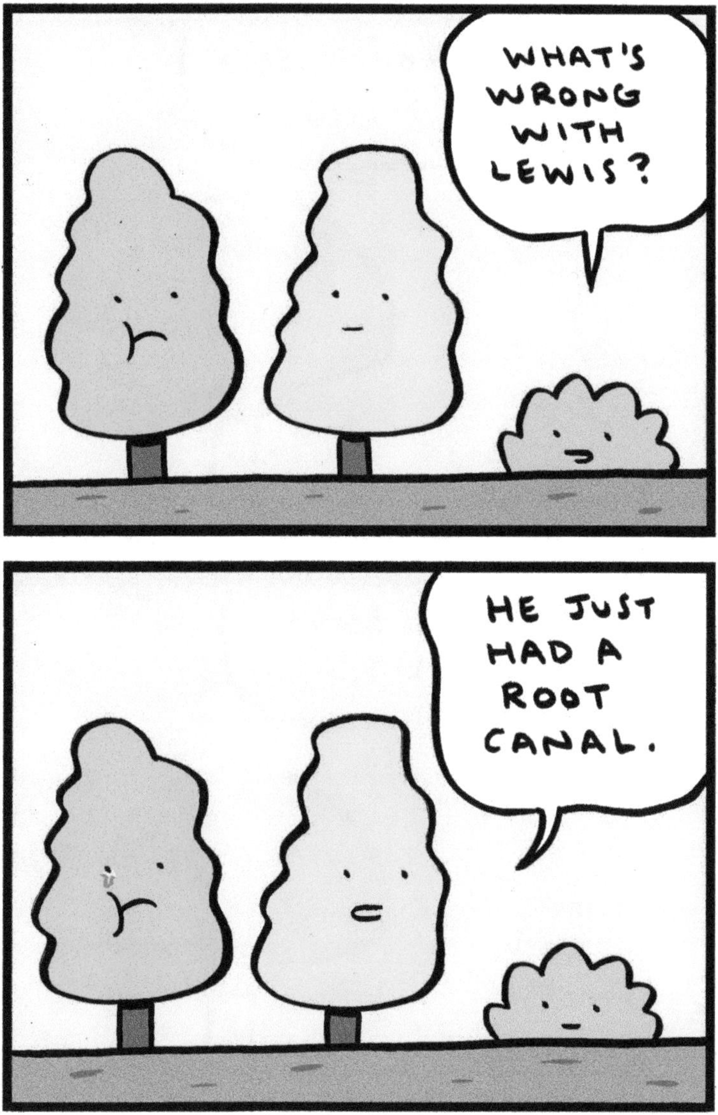
WHAT'S WRONG WITH LEWIS?
HE JUST HAD A ROOT CANAL.

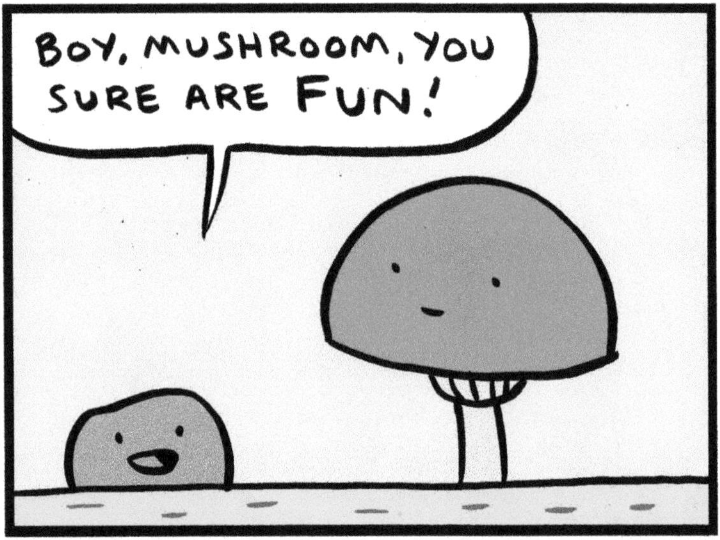
BOY, MUSHROOM, YOU SURE ARE FUN!

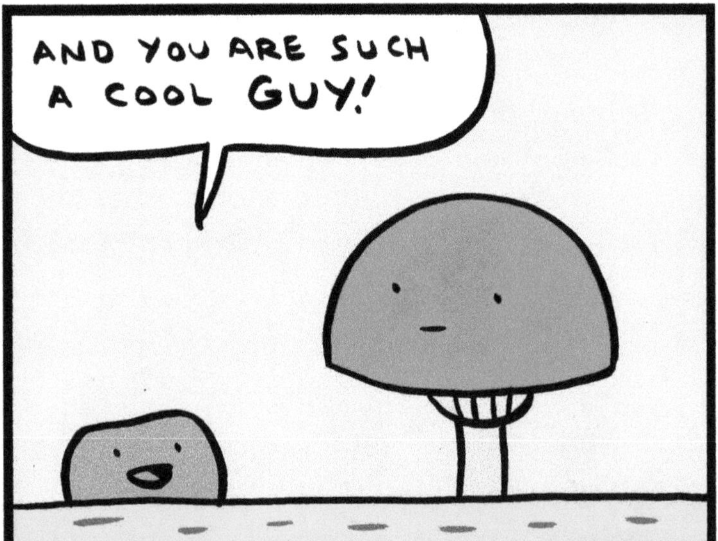
AND YOU ARE SUCH A COOL GUY!

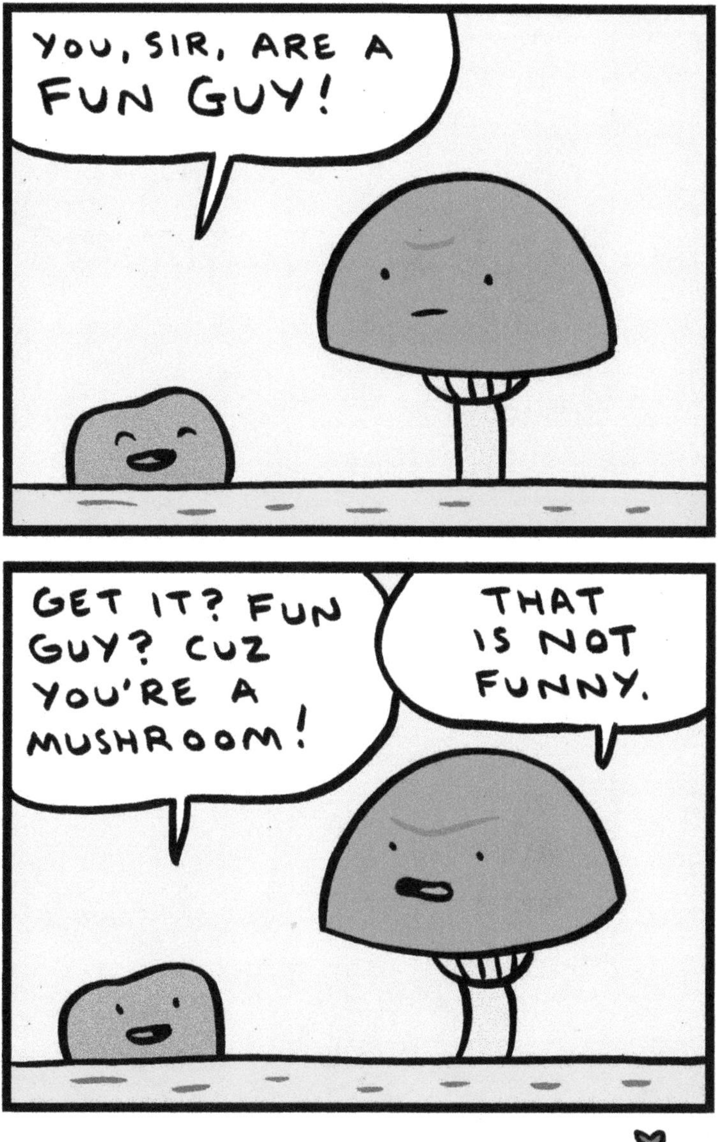
YOU, SIR, ARE A FUN GUY!
GET IT? FUN GUY? CUZ YOU'RE A MUSHROOM!
THAT IS NOT FUNNY.

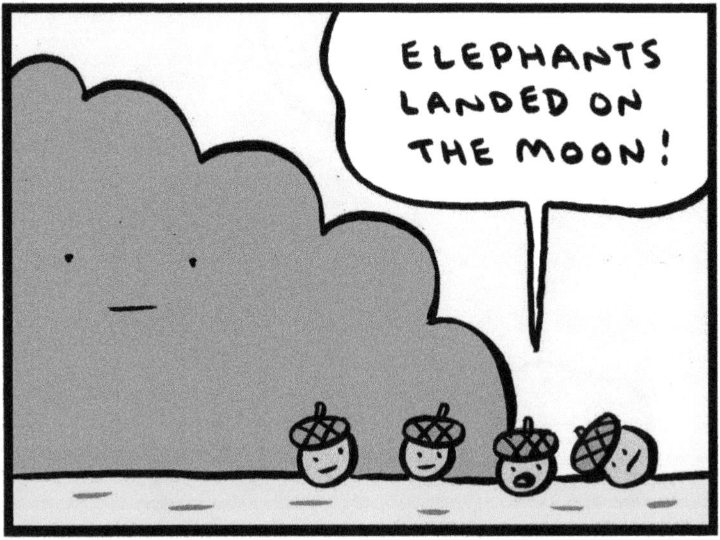
ELEPHANTS LANDED ON THE MOON!

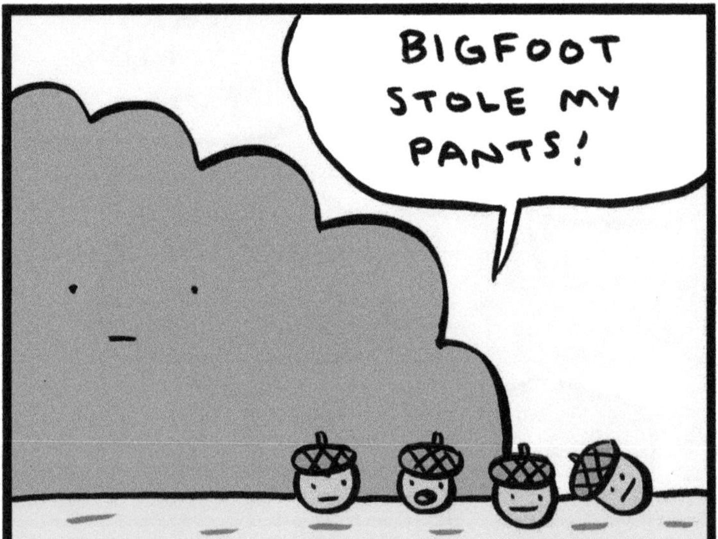
BIGFOOT STOLE MY PANTS!

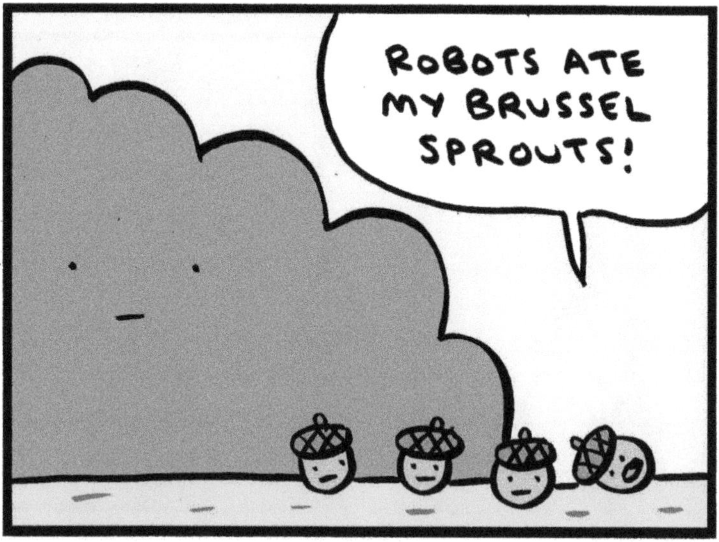
ROBOTS ATE MY BRUSSEL SPROUTS!

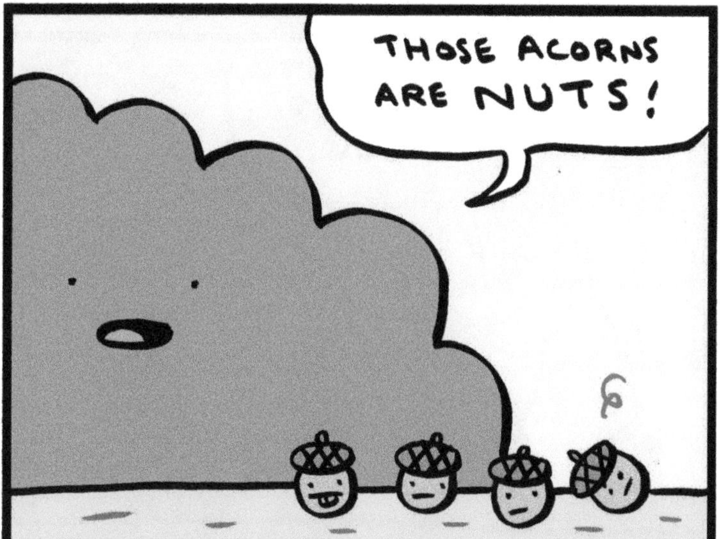
THOSE ACORNS ARE NUTS!

TRENDSETTER

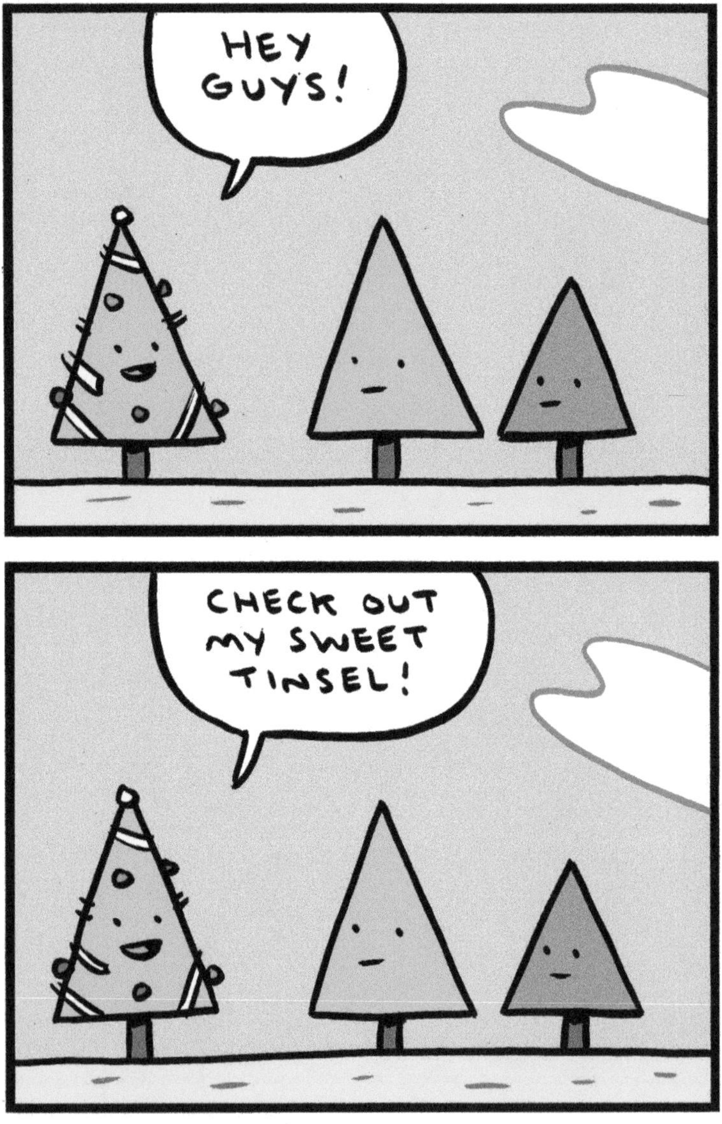
HEY GUYS!
CHECK OUT MY SWEET TINSEL!

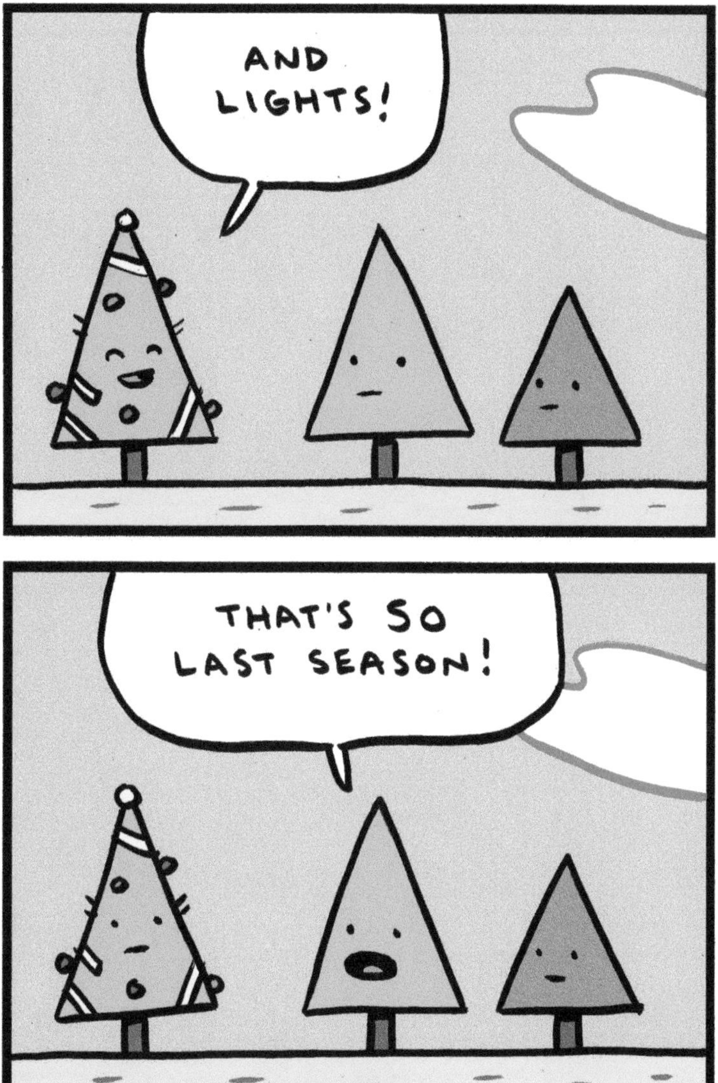
AND LIGHTS!
THAT'S SO LAST SEASON!

OLD MAN ELM

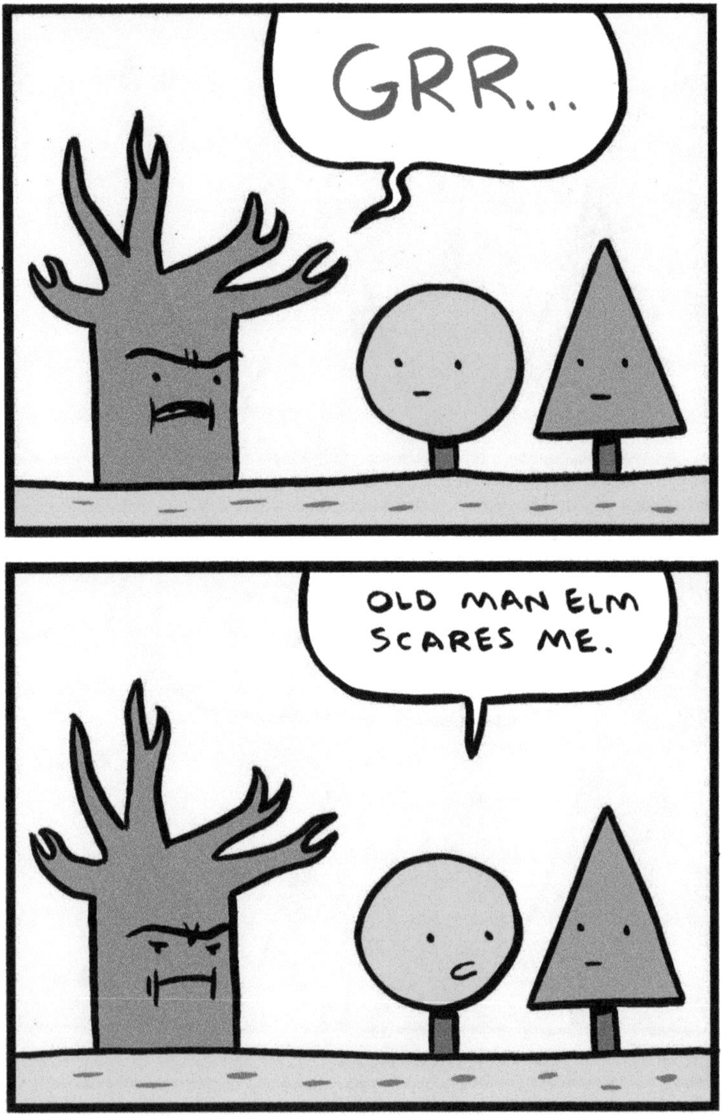
GRR...
OLD MAN ELM SCARES ME.

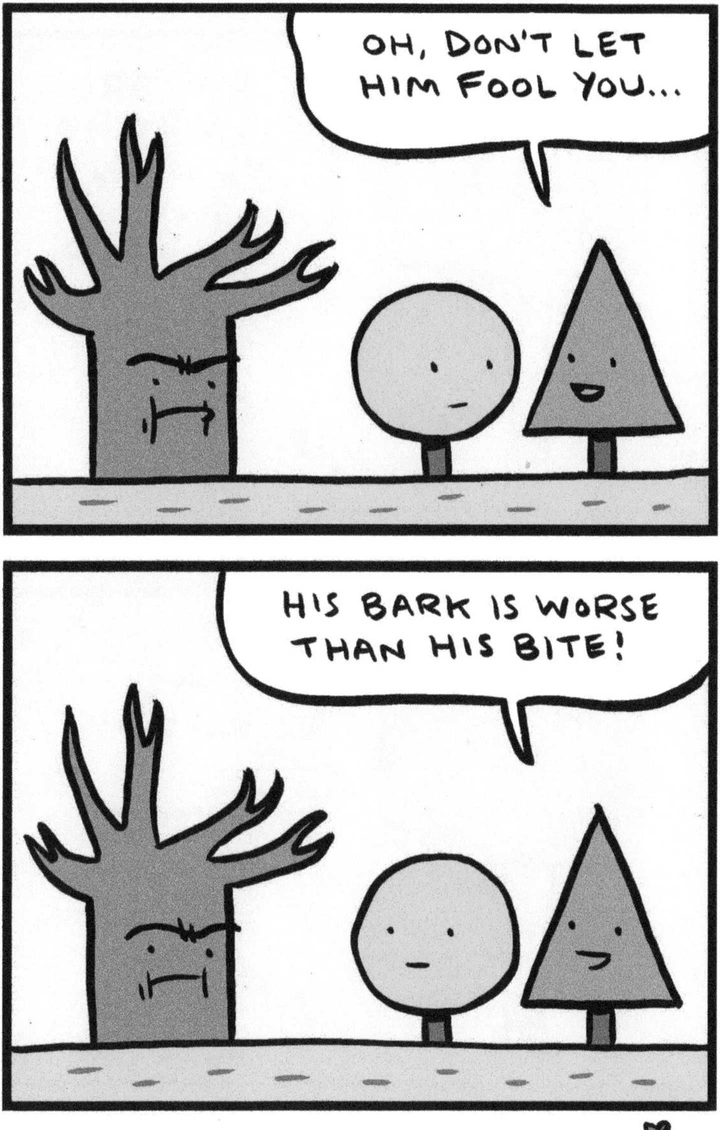
OH, DON'T LET HIM FOOL YOU...
HIS BARK IS WORSE THAN HIS BITE!

WEATHER

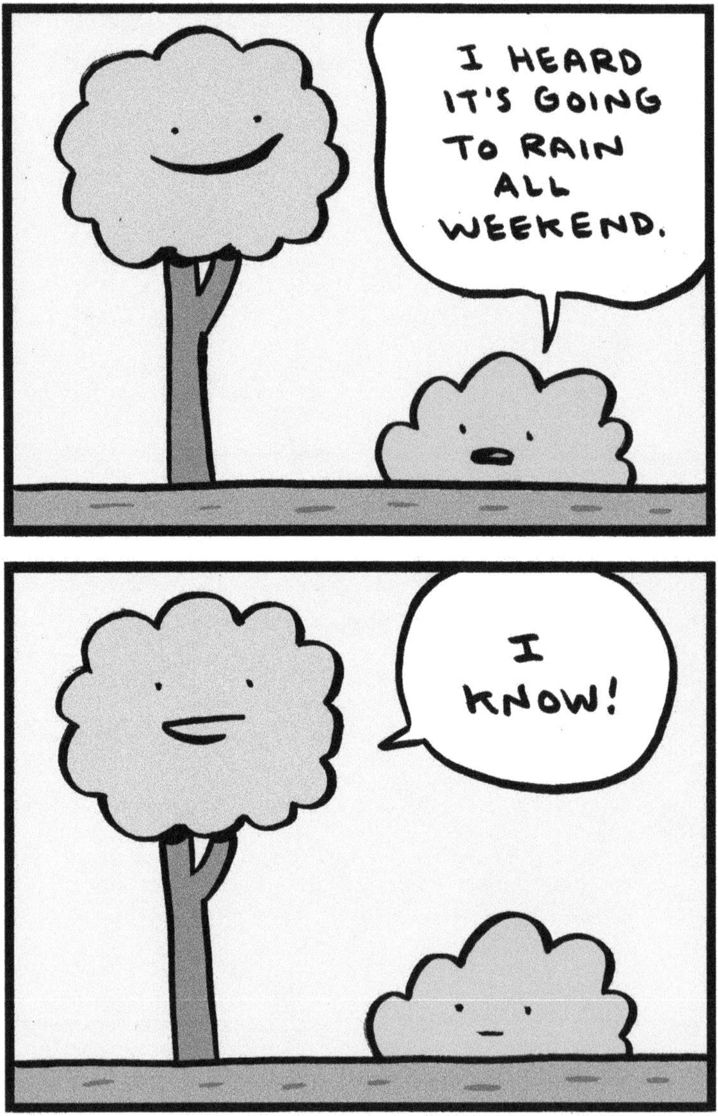
I HEARD IT'S GOING TO RAIN ALL WEEKEND.
I KNOW!

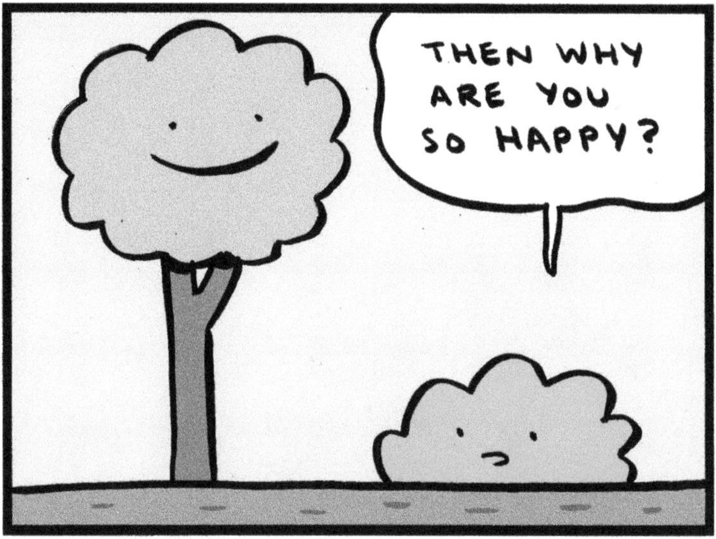
THEN WHY ARE YOU SO HAPPY?

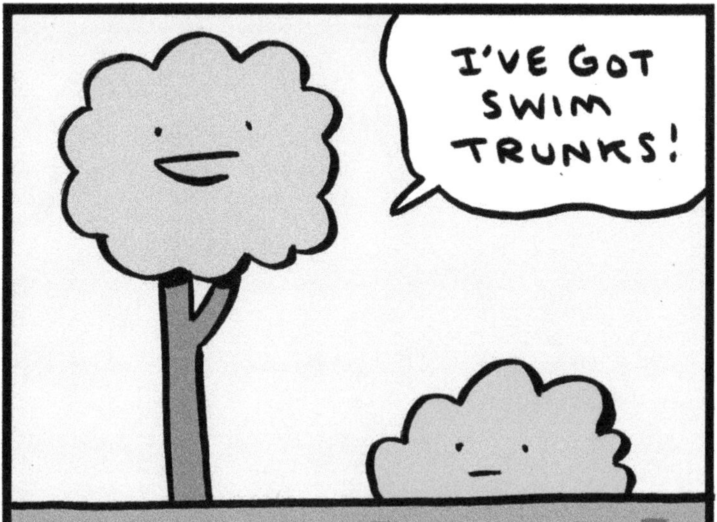
I'VE GOT SWIM TRUNKS!

TWINS

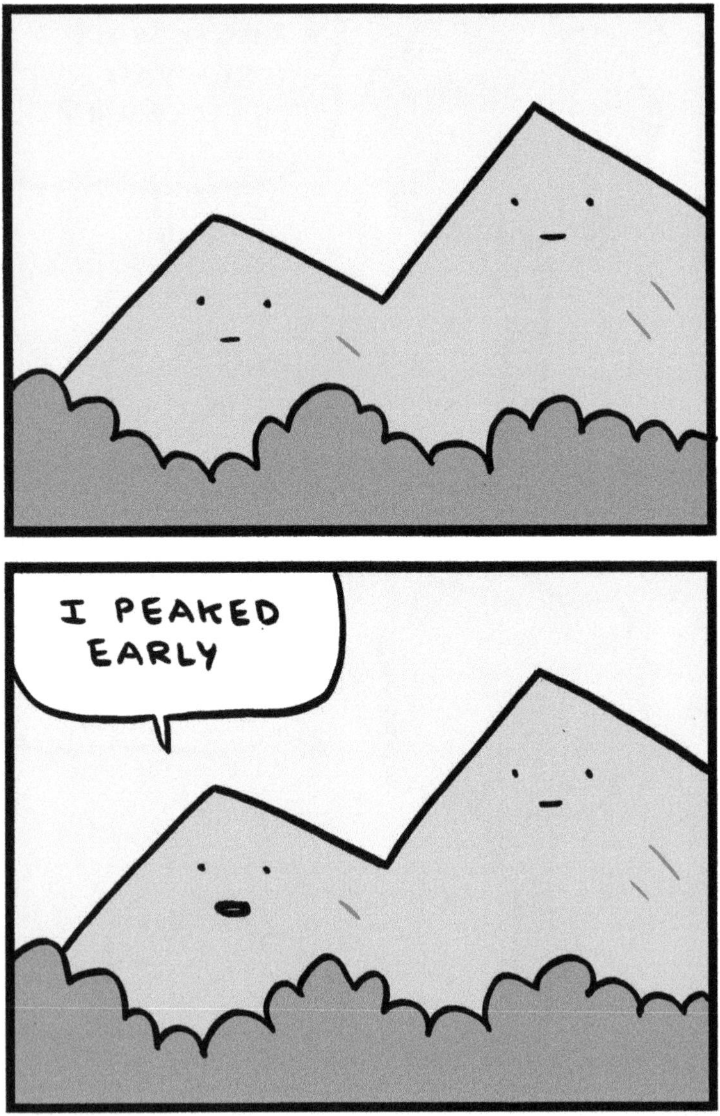
I PEAKED EARLY

CARL

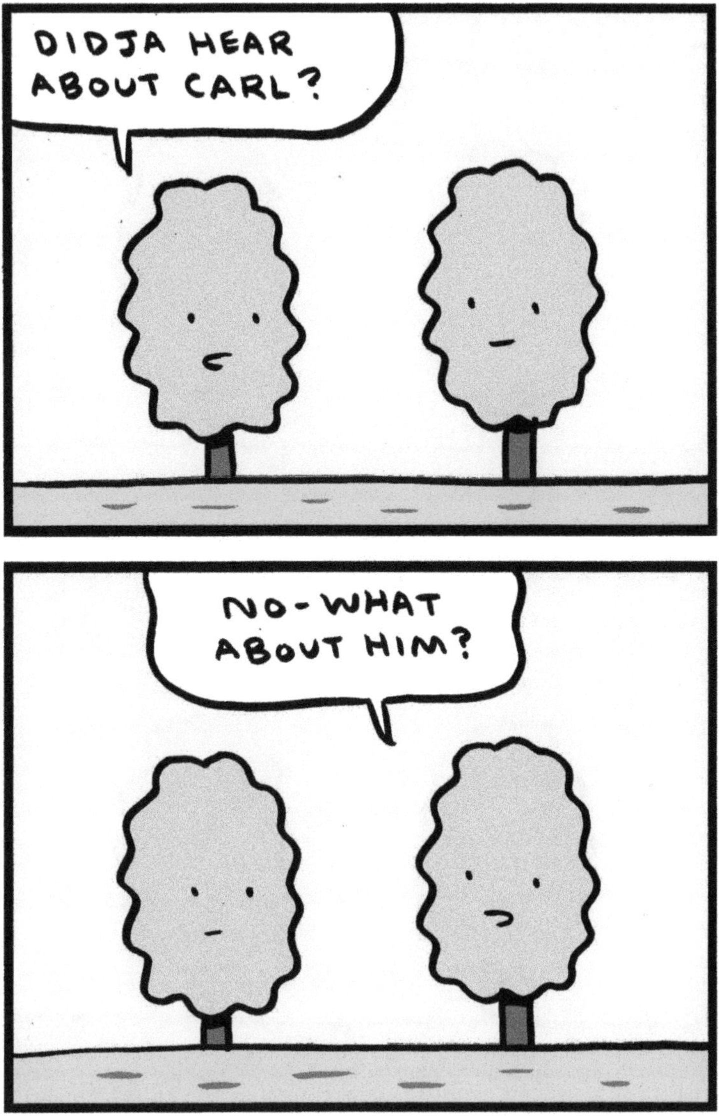
DIDJA HEAR ABOUT CARL?
NO-WHAT ABOUT HIM?

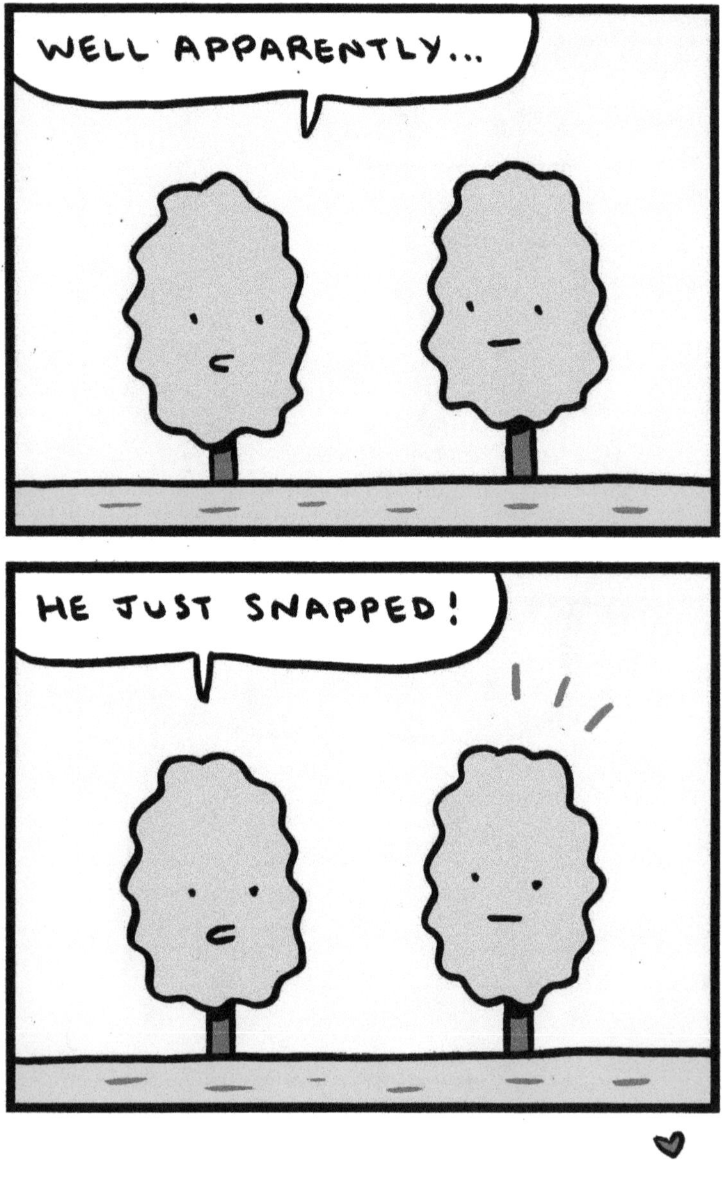
WELL APPARENTLY...
HE JUST SNAPPED!

Todd Webb was born in 1981.
He lives in Virginia with his wife and their cat.
He likes to sit outside and birch trees are his favorite.

Other works include *The Goldfish & Bob*,
Tuesday Moon, *Casual Poet*,
Robbert Bobbert & the Bubble Machine,
Chance Operations, *Minor Changes*,
The Adventures of Danny & Mike,
and *Mr Toast Comics*. Webb performs music as
Seamonster, and is always drawing.

To keep up with Todd or say hello, visit:
www.toddbot.com

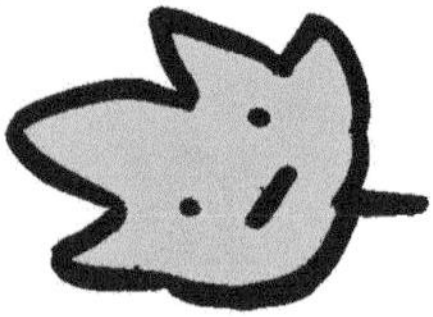

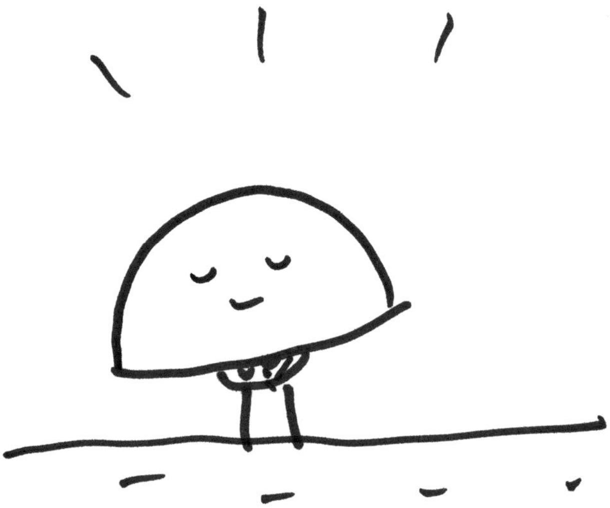

♡ todd! 2019

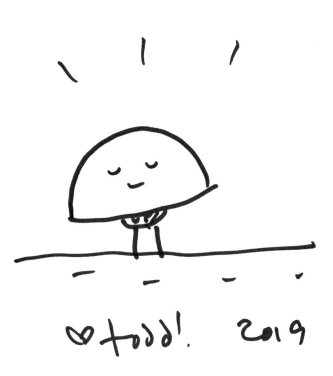

CPSIA information can be obtained
at www.ICGtesting.com
Printed in the USA
BVHW060822210219
540789BV00004B/12/P